The Terrace Builders of Nyanga

Robert Soper

WEAVER

—PRESS—

Published by Weaver Press, P.O. Box A1922, Avondale, Harare. 2006

Typeset by: TextPertise, Harare
Cover Design: Xealos Harare
Cover photographs: Robert Soper
Printed by: Sable Press, Harare

The Archaeology Unit at the University of Zimbabwe would like to express its gratitude to NUFU,
the Norwegian Programme for Development, Research and Higher Education,
for their support in the research and publication of this title.

The author and publisher would also like to acknowledge
The British Institute in Eastern Africa
for permission to reproduce all the illustrations other than Fig. 11.

ISBN-10: 1-77922-061-8
ISBN-13: 978-1-77922-061-5

Contents

List of Illustrations   *iv*

Preface   *v*

Acknowledgements   *vi*

About the author   *vi*

Chapter 1:

      The Nyanga Complex   **1**

Chapter 2:

      Settlement Sites and the Development of the Complex   **11**

Chapter 3:

      Agricultural Works and Water Management   **43**

Chapter 4:

      Agricultural Economy   **61**

Chapter 5:

      Society in the Nyanga Complex   **69**

Appendix: Radiocarbon Dates for Nyanga Sites   *78*

Annotated References for Further Reading   *80*

List of illustrations

Fig. 1:   Map of the Nyanga area 2

Fig. 2:   Dense terracing near foot of the escarpment north of Nyautare 3

Fig. 3:   Mouth of tunnel into a pit, Nyangui site G1/21 4

Fig. 4:   Grave cut through the cobbled floor of a walled hollow, Nyangui 1732DD27 15

Fig. 5:   Grassy hollow of a ruined pit-structure 16

Fig. 6:   Pit and entrance passage with stone paving and revetment, Matinha 17

Fig. 7:   Plan of pit-structure, National Park 18

Fig. 8:   Pit-structure with restored houses, National Park..19

Fig. 9:   Plan of a divided house, National Park 21

Fig. 10: Plan of a pit-enclosure, Ziwa 24

Fig. 11: Rock gong at Ziwa...25

Fig. 12: Plan of a double concentric enclosure appended to a residential enclosure, Chigura 26

Fig. 13: Mount Muozi from the east side of the saddle 28

Fig. 14: Muozi. Plan of the stone ruins on the western promontory 29

Fig. 15: Muozi. House circles with the main group of complete pots 30

Fig. 16: Iron object from Muozi 31

Fig. 17: Chirangeni. Plan of the enclosure...33

Fig. 18: Sketch plan of Mujinga fort, Ziwa 38

Fig. 19: Three types of iron-smelting furnaces 40

Fig. 20: Furnace of type 1, middle Pungwe valley, National Park 41

Fig. 21: Two hoes found in digging a pipe trench at Ziwa 42

Fig. 22: Distribution of terracing identified from aerial photographs 44

Fig. 23: Plan of terracing and enclosures at Ziwa 46

Fig. 24: Section of terrace transect, Ziwa 47

Fig. 25: Granite terracing, Chirangeni 48

Fig. 26: Cultivation ridges north of Maristvale: aerial photograph 51

Fig. 27: Footpath following old furrow, Demera hill 55

Fig. 28: National Park looking north-east: Furrow 4 traverses the slope in the middle distance 58

Preface

Many readers in Zimbabwe approaching this book will be familiar with at least some of the Nyanga ruins and will have speculated on their meaning. Most, however, will not be aware of their full range and extent, nor of their age and what they represent. The ruins have been described and discussed for more than a century and have given rise to various fanciful interpretations, some of which still appear to have some adherents. The sober facts may be less romantic but are no less interesting in documenting the achievements of the ancient inhabitants.

The results of extensive research conducted between 1993 and 1999 have recently been published as an archaeological monograph (Soper, 2002), which sets out in full the detailed evidence and technical analysis, and argues the interpretation at some length. Many people will find this treatment quite tedious, and this less technical account is offered as more palatable to the interested but less academic reader.

The stone ruins and other cultural remains associated with them include a wide range of features: stone-faced terracing covering escarpments, hills or valley slopes; extensive areas of cultivation ridges; water furrows; mountain-top settlement clusters; stone-built homesteads such as 'pit-structures' and various types of enclosures, which differ according to altitude and area; defensive structures or 'forts'; and iron-smelting sites.

The best known features of the ruins are in Nyanga National Park, where Nyangwe and Chawomera forts and the restored pit-structure are seen by hundreds of visitors every year. Other pit-structures are also signposted in several places. Less obvious to the casual eye are the old water furrows, but one is clearly visible from Chawomera fort to the east across the Nyangombe river, while another good example can be seen beyond the Nyamziwa river to the right as the road descends to the Falls.

There is little obvious terracing to be seen in the Park itself, as most of this is found at lower altitudes. To see this it is best to visit the Ziwa National Monument, 25 kilometres north-west from Nyanga village. This is one of the densest concentrations of terracing, stone homestead enclosures and other features in the whole of Nyanga. At first glance – indeed at second and subsequent glances – they present a bewildering maze of stone walls, staggering testimony to the industry of the ancient inhabitants. They are described and explained at the excellent Site Museum, the custodians of which will assist with a brief guided tour. More adventurous visitors may, with due precautions, wander extensively through the 33 square kilometres of the Monument. Camping facilities are available at the Museum.

The restored pit-structure in the National Park (Fig. 8) gives a good impression of the design of one type of homestead, although the addition of some tiny cows in the pit, and goats, people and children around the houses, would enliven the picture. The construction of the houses is consistent with excavated evidence, but the interior arrangements are not, apart from the slot in the floor of the main house opening into the tunnel. A more authentic house type would be divided by a low wall across the middle, with kitchen on one side and goats on the other, as described in Chapter 2.

The summit of World's View is also visited by many people and the walls of the early hilltop settlement can be seen around the highest point, although much is difficult to trace in the low, dense thickets.

The old grain bins in caves and the stone walls which are found among many hills and rocks from the Juliasdale area westwards have not yet been the object of any systematic archaeological research and will not be discussed in this book. They are probably to be attributed to the Manyika in the 19th century as more or less hidden settlements or strategic refuges in time of danger. We cannot yet say for certain whether the pit-structures that are often found in the same areas are of the same date: from the relative state of preservation they seem likely to be earlier.

While a general picture of the archaeology of the Nyanga ruins is now apparent, this cannot claim to be a final comprehensive account. Many areas have not been investigated in detail, if at all, and many questions remain to be answered. The recent research has concentrated mainly on the area north of Nyanga town, and within that on certain areas, especially Ziwa ruins, Maristvale, Nyautare, Ruangwe, Kagore, parts of Nyangui Forest land, and Chirimanyimo. Even here not all the remains have been visited and recorded. Similarly, excavations have been on a relatively small scale, aimed at a sample of terraces and of typical homesteads for dating purposes and to reveal the houses and other structures within them. Future work will clarify and expand the picture – and doubtless modify some of the conclusions.

Acknowledgements

Grateful acknowledgement is due to many bodies and individuals too numerous to mention who facilitated the recent research. This was a joint project between the British Institute in Eastern Africa and the History Department of the University of Zimbabwe in close co-operation with the National Museums and Monuments of Zimbabwe, largely funded by the Rhodes Trustees and the British Academy. I am especially grateful to John Sutton, who initiated the research project and has provided advice and constructive criticism throughout from his wide knowledge of African terracing and field systems, while his comments on drafts of the original monograph offered many cogent suggestions for its improvement.

The figures, with the exception of Fig. 11, are reproduced with the permission of The British Institute in Eastern Africa.

About the author

Robert Soper began his teaching and research in Africa in 1962 and he has worked in Nigeria, East Africa and Zimbabwe. His interests have ranged from Early Farming Communities in East Africa, to excavations at the ancient Yoruba capital of Old Oyo in Nigeria, to a survey of the still operating traditional irrigation systems of the Marakwet of Kenya.

He joined the History Department at the University of Zimbabwe in 1985 and was involved in establishing their archaeology teaching programme. After excavation of the Great Zimbabwe tradition sites in Centenary, from 1993 he directed the research project 'Archaeology and Agricultural History in Nyanga' studying the terraces and other agricultural works and the communities responsible for them. He retired from the University of Zimbabwe in 2006.

CHAPTER 1
The Nyanga Complex

The complex and its builders

The ruined stone structures of Nyanga and neighbouring districts represent probably the largest complex of ancient building in Africa. They are a major testament to the energy and ingenuity of the past inhabitants of a large area of north-eastern Zimbabwe (Fig. 1). In many areas the impressive stone-faced terraces have modified whole landscapes, covering every hill and valley side in ranges of up to 100 successive steps (Fig. 2), while hundreds of hectares of valley soils have been worked into wide cultivation ridges. Associated with these are the stone-built homesteads of the builders and, in many areas, their defensive forts or refuges. Old water furrows demonstrate their utilisation of available water resources, and traces of iron-working show their industrial activities.

The main distribution of the terracing itself (Fig. 22) extends from Ruangwe in the north to the Pungwe valley in the south, to the Cumberland valley/Burnaby in the south-west and into Tanda/Chinyika west of the Nyangombe river, a total area of some 5,000 square kilometres. Lesser outlying occurrences are reported in the Makaha area of Mutoko, west to Headlands/Weya and south in Chimanimani. The situation in Mozambique is unclear much beyond the immediate valley of the Gairezi. Pit-structure homesteads typical of the higher areas of the complex extend somewhat further beyond the terrace distribution, almost to Penhalonga in the south, and west along the main watershed to the Lesapi area. Probably related are walled villages with lintelled entrances in the area north-east of Rusape – for example, at Diana's Vow and the Chitakete site at Harleigh Farm.

The whole complex represents an agricultural society of industrious farmers and stock-raisers whose culture developed from about AD 1300 to sometime in the 19th century. Much of the latter part of this time range falls within the scope of the present chiefdoms of the region – Saunyama, Mutasa and Makoni – and there is little doubt that the complex is the achievement of the ancestors of the present populations, although little memory of it seems to survive.

People frequently wonder why such enormous labour was expended on terracing the stony slopes and escarpments when there was plenty of land on the plateaux and in the lowlands which could be far more easily exploited. Some writers have speculated that the builders were forced into an unfavourable environment as a defensive reaction to stronger antagonistic neighbours. This might be understandable for the highlands and even the escarpments, but it could hardly apply to the low hills in the plains, which in no sense could provide a secure refuge. We may therefore look for other reasons for exploiting the slopes, of which the most likely is their relative fertility.

The plateau soils of the highlands are deep and well drained, but are strongly leached owing to high rainfall and thus almost devoid of mineral nutrients essential for cultivation. The original vegetation may well have been mountain forest, the clearance of which would have provided fertility for a year or two from the organic

1

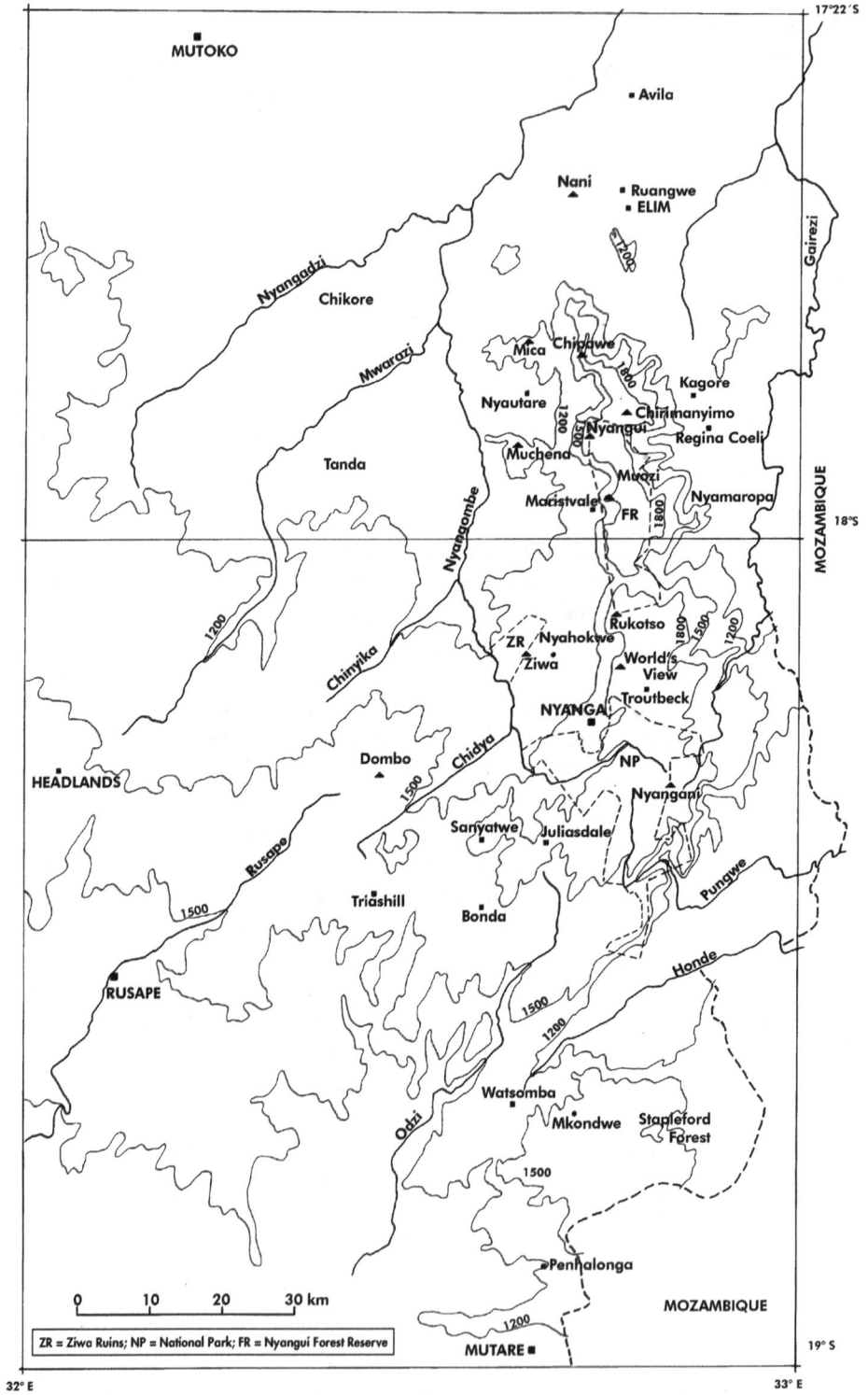

Fig. 1: Map of the Nyanga area

nutrients. However, once these had been squandered in the earlier stages of the complex, the soils were only fit for the short grassland which they now support. Modern farming in the highlands – for instance, for potato cultivation – involves the use of artificial fertilisers, while the early farmers appear to have used manure on small localised gardens only. The soils of lowlands and valleys, more or less stoneless, are generally sandy and also of limited fertility. They were, however, very extensively exploited by means of broad ridging, as will be shown in Chapter 3.

Terrace construction favoured the dolerite rocks and soils, both on the escarpments and on the hills within the plains. The soils of the slopes, while often shallow and stony, are young and unleached and retain much of their mineral nutrients – which, indeed, are slowly regenerated through the ongoing decomposition of the parent rock which weathers relatively rapidly. Terracing clears the stones and concentrates and conserves the sparse soil, while impeding run-off to allow good percolation of water. Farmers are always keenly aware of relative soil fertility and how it can best be managed, and in this case they clearly recognised the potential of the local conditions and considered them worth the labour to exploit.

The extensive use of stone in the construction of homesteads has been plausibly attributed to the scarcity of suitable timber, especially in the highlands. Stone had to be used wherever possible, with any straight poles being kept for roofing, while other timber was doubtless needed for fencing gardens against wild

Fig. 2: Dense terracing near foot of the escarpment north of Nyautare

and domestic animals. Stone walls were not, however, a mere direct substitute for wooden fences or wall frames but are integral to the design of the homesteads. The manipulation of stones must have been an everyday activity of most members of the community.

At first glance much of the stonework appears crude in comparison with the more regular architecture of Great Zimbabwe, but this is a misconception. The available stones – mostly dolerite, granite or sandstone – occur in irregular shapes varying in size from small fragments to slabs and boulders weighing several hundred kilograms (Fig. 3). To fit these into a stable structure requires more skill than for the granite of Great Zimbabwe, which breaks up into regular blocks. The faces of the Nyanga walls were constructed of larger stones carefully fitted and wedged, while smaller stones were used to fill the core of the wall; no mortar was used. The survival of many of the structures in basically sound condition is an indication of the quality of the work. Moreover, the vast number of terraces and buildings were all the work of the ordinary people to achieve their everyday needs. In contrast, the Great Zimbabwe stone buildings were prestige architecture of a dominant minority. This fundamental difference in architecture is one aspect which shows of the lack of relationship between the Nyanga and Great Zimbabwe cultures, emphasised by other aspects such as different pottery styles.

Fig. 3: Mouth of tunnel into a pit, Nyangui site G1/21

What was the relationship between the people responsible for the Nyanga structures and other contemporary peoples of the region and even perhaps further afield? Where did they come from? Did they invent the terracing, bring the idea with them, or learn it from somebody else?

Terracing is not uncommon in Africa where appropriate conditions exist – steep, stony slopes and some motive for cultivating them. Notable examples are found in eastern Mpumalanga (Eastern Transvaal) and in the Konso area of south-western Ethiopia. Even though there are similarities to Nyanga in the terraces and the stone-walled passageways through them, these can be explained as parallel responses to similar conditions and needs, and there is no reason to postulate any direct relationship: there are limited ways in which stony slopes can be effectively exploited for cultivation.

Who, then, were the builders? As we shall see, we can trace a sequence of development of the complex from around AD 1300 to the forebears of the present peoples of the area – Nyama, Manyika and perhaps Maungwe – who now speak dialects of Shona but may not all have done so in earlier times. This development sequence parallels in time much of the Zimbabwe archaeological culture, which represents the Zimbabwe state itself and the succeeding Torwa, Changamire and Mutapa states. The Zimbabwe culture as a whole can be confidently attributed to the emergence and spread of Shona speakers.

However, we have seen the clear cultural distinction of the Nyanga archaeological evidence from that of the Great Zimbabwe culture, showing that the basic Nyanga populations were not originally related to the Shona. Nor, according to the archaeological evidence, were they obviously related to other Later Farming Community peoples of Zimbabwe. Earlier workers in Nyanga attributed the ruins to Sena speakers, part of a linguistic group found in Mozambique to the east, whose language seems to have influenced the current dialects. On the other hand, the political ruling dynasties of the area – Saunyama, Mutasa, Makoni – claim to have come from 'Nembire', usually identified with the Shona-speaking Mutapa state. While these may be legitimising myths not to be taken too literally, they at least reflect Shona origins. Such dynasties are recorded by the Portuguese for Manyika and Maungwe by the 16th century, while the genealogies of Saunyama dynasties extend back at least to the 18th century. As we shall see in Chapter 5, the distribution of the Nyanga complex and local variations within it do not correspond to the present territories of these chiefdoms or any known earlier territorial changes to them. Thus it looks as if the political superstructure was imposed on a pre-existing cultural substratum, resulting in a process of linguistic 'Shona-isation'. Whether this substratum was Sena-speaking is probably not now possible to establish, but it is at least plausible.

The impression is that the people of the Nyanga complex were relatively isolated from neighbouring peoples. The records of the Portuguese, who interacted extensively with the Mutapa kingdom to the west and also with the Manyika immediately to the south, do not mention the Nyanga area, which suggests that it was of little political importance. This is consistent with a relatively small total population, as deduced from historical and archaeological evidence. There are almost no exotic objects, beyond generally rare glass beads, to suggest that the Nyanga people participated directly in any trading networks. However, a few isolated sherds of Great Zimbabwe-type pottery at two or three sites show that there was some local interaction with their neighbours.

The Nyanga environment

Any society is strongly shaped by the way in which it chooses to adapt to the potentials and constraints of its physical environment. This is particularly so in the Nyanga case, where the specialised techniques of terracing, ridging and water management were finely tuned to the opportunities offered by the landscape (Fig. 1).

Topography

The complex occupies the northern part of Zimbabwe's Eastern Highlands. Here a broad plateau narrows northwards into a high range flanked by steep escarpments to the east and west, with lower, drier plains either side.

South and east of Nyanga town is the broad dissected plateau at around 1,800m above sea level and about 15km wide. This rises to the east to Mount Nyangani, at 2,592m the highest point in Zimbabwe, while beyond the land drops steeply to the Mozambique border. The plateau is largely occupied by the Nyanga National Park and extends south-west to Juliasdale and west to Sanyatwe. Thence it declines relatively gently to the west past Triashill to merge with the main watershed between the Zambezi and Save basins at around 1,500m, which continues through Headlands and Macheke. To the south the plateau is terminated by the Honde and Odzi valleys, but the country rises again to a further plateau at 1,600m to 1,800m, rising in the east to Stapleford Forest at 2,000m.

North of Nyanga town the broad plateau narrows somewhat through the Nyanga Downs to form a narrower plateau only a few kilometres wide at around 2,000m, and this continues northwards for about 50km, broken by the Bende Gap, a lower pass at about 1,750m. This narrow plateau is crowned along its western edge by a series of peaks at 2,200m to 2,400m: World's View, Rukotso, Chinyamaura, Nyangui, Chirimanyimo and Chipawe. It is bordered to the east and west by steep escarpments, often with near vertical cliffs, the western escarpment being around 600m high and the eastern somewhat lower. A number of major spurs project to east and west, of which the most prominent is Muozi. The Ruangwe range extends for another 25km northwards at a lower altitude of 1,100m to 1,200m, with a steep escarpment on its eastern side.

To the west of this high range are relatively flat lowlands broken by granite inselbergs and kopjes and lesser dolerite features, traversed by the broad Nyangombe valley. This landscape continues across the Nyangombe through Tanda and Chinyika Communal Lands. East of the high range the country drops to the Gairezi river and to the north-east is the Matisi basin, generally flat country with granite features.

Drainage radiates from Mount Nyangani, where most of the main rivers rise. The Pungwe runs steeply south and then east to the Indian Ocean. The Nyangombe drops west off the plateau and then turns north parallel to the highland range, becoming the Ruenya and joining the Zambezi. The Gairezi falls steeply to the north-east, then turns north along the Mozambique border to join the Ruenya. The Odzi rises further to the south-west and flows south-west to join the Save.

The favourable rainfall in the highlands gives rise to numerous permanent streams that descend the escarpments at steep gradients or wind through the deep valleys of the main plateau. The ample water flow and steep gradients facilitate diversion into artificial furrows, directing the water to where it may have been needed, either in the highlands or on the footslopes of the escarpments. Water furrows are discussed in Chapter 3. On the plateau the streams are often flanked by more or less waterlogged alluvial or peaty deposits. On the footslopes below the escarpments, seasonally waterlogged vleis or even substantial bogs have formed where drainage is at all impeded, while vleis are also found in the lowland valleys. Some such areas were exploited by the large cultivation ridges, while their use has continued to recent times by the construction of shorter, straighter and steeper ridges called *mihomba*.

Within this topography, the Nyanga complex area may be conceived as divided into two zones, highlands and lowlands, at the 1,400m contour. ('Lowlands' is, of course, a relative term, since much of this zone lies above 1,000m.) A cultural distinction is evident at this level. While terracing is common to both the lowland zone and the highland zone up to about 1,700m, the design of homesteads differs, with typical pit-structures occurring only above 1,400m and various forms of enclosures below, as described in Chapter 2. This cultural distinction remains to be explained. The division coincides approximately with the base of the escarpments either side of the northern range, but there does not appear to be a correlation with any obvious topographical or present vegetational distinction elsewhere, so that an environmental cause is hard to maintain. There may be a relationship with past climatic differences, discussed below, possibly heavy winter frosts or drier conditions which may have prevailed around the 18th century in the final phase of what has been called the 'Little Ice Age'.

Geology

This area of the Eastern Highlands is composed of granites overlain by sedimentary rocks and dolerites. Terracing and settlement are found on all three rock types, but the terracing at least favours the dolerites.

The granitic rocks are the most extensive and form most of the western lowlands, often relatively flat but broken by granite hills and kopjes, which may be large features such as Ziwa and Muchena. The granites are overlain by sedimentary rocks such as sandstones, siltstones and shales. Igneous dolerites in the form of either vertical dykes or horizontal sheets or sills have intruded both granites and sediments, overlying or penetrating between the earlier strata. The sedimentary rocks and dolerites cap much of the highlands north of the Bende Gap and form the northward extension of the Ruangwe range, where they are folded into a series of parallel ridges and valleys. West of the highlands, dolerite sills and dykes form low, boulder-covered hills and narrow ridges within the granite terrain, and most of these are terraced.

There is alluvium on the banks of the larger rivers, especially the Gairezi and Nyangombe, but the only extensive alluvial deposits are in the area of the Nyamaropa irrigation scheme and the Nyarawaka basin to the north-west of this.

Iron ore in the form of black magnetite sand has been weathered from the dolerite, as can be clearly seen around Ziwa Site Museum. This appears to have been used in the smelting furnaces in the Ziwa/Nyahokwe and Nyanga town/ National Park areas (Chapter 2) while laterite was probably used at other smelting sites in the north-east.

Gold is not found in the main Nyanga area but is common in the Makaha Gold Belt to the north in Mutoko District. Sporadic terracing and stone ruins occur in this area, but it is unclear how they relate to the Nyanga complex. Some copper and traces of tin also occur in the Makaha Gold belt, while Inyati copper mine north-east of Headlands falls within the western extension of sporadic terracing. Mineral exploitation apart from iron was thus not an important feature of the complex.

Soils

Soils and their inherent fertility are a controlling factor for agricultural production and are thus critical in the consideration of terracing and other agricultural works. Nyanga soils are very diverse owing to varying conditions of geology, topography and climate. On the highland plateaux the soils are deep but infertile, being very weathered and leached by the high rainfall, with high acidity. In the lowlands there is less weathering and leaching. Here soils derived from dolerite are deep, red and clayey with good chemical fertility and are probably the most productive soils in Zimbabwe. The granitic soils are mostly sandy with little inherent fertility apart from organic matter. The stony slope soils of the dolerite escarpments and hills have not been subjected to deep weathering and are thus immature, retaining a higher proportion of mineral nutrients. Their relative fertility has already been noted as the probable stimulus for the Nyanga terracing.

Climate

Nyanga enjoys a moderate climate with fair rainfall, but with marked seasonality and a long dry season in the middle of the year. Almost all rainfall occurs between November and March. The highest areas may also receive some mist or drizzle in the winter months. Average annual rainfall varies largely with altitude. Averages in the highlands generally are around 900 mm to 1,150 mm per year, reaching over 1,400 mm in the highest areas. In the lowlands averages are around 700 mm to 900 mm. There is wide annual variation, not uncommonly up to plus or minus 50 per cent, and there may be considerable local differences in any one year.

Higher altitudes experience very cold winds and hard frosts in winter but below about 1,500 m these are not a serious problem for most areas. The wet-season cloud-base gives dense mists above about 1,900 m which may persist for days at a time, and this has discouraged settlement.

Available information on long-term climatic trends suggests cold and probably dry conditions between AD 1300 and 1500, warmer/wetter conditions to about 1675, and cooler/drier again to about 1850 (the 'Little Ice Age'), followed by amelioration to the present. Most of the evidence for this comes from South Africa, and the effects were probably less severe and the colder phases more curtailed in north-eastern Zimbabwe.

Vegetation

There is a considerable range of vegetation types, as might be expected from the variation in altitude, climate and soils. Five broad vegetation types have been distinguished:

1. Evergreen mountain forest in the high rainfall areas south and east of Mount Nyangani and the Pungwe Gorge but largely cleared elsewhere to leave types 3 and 4.
2. Bracken scrub in western areas of the National Park and the southern plateau, much of it now covered with pine plantations. Apart from the bracken there are coarse, tufted grasses, woody shrubs and small trees, with clumps of forest, especially in and around old pit-structures.
3. Short open grassland in the eastern parts of the National Park and northwards through Nyanga Downs and along the northern highlands. This has a dense grass sward around 50 cm high with a variety of herbs and few trees. Large areas of the northern highlands are now covered by the pine plantations of Nyangui Forest.
4. *Brachystegia–Julbernardia* (*msasa*) woodland in the higher areas to west of the bracken scrub above about 1,400 m, extending northwards, fringing the short grassland and on the escarpments.
5. Mixed woodland in the Nyangombe basin and other lower areas below about 1,400 m. This is generally sparse on arable land but is quite dense on hillsides and rocky areas. Baobabs become increasingly common north of Maristvale as conditions get drier.

There has been little archaeological research in the areas of type 1. Stone walls do occur in dense forest around Mount Nyangani and on Chirimanyimo but are hard to trace; it may be assumed that the forest has regenerated since they were abandoned. Pit-structures are common in areas of types 2 and 3 where terraces are rare or absent. Terracing is common on the escarpments and lower areas (types 4 and 5), with pit-structures also associated with type 4 and various other kinds of stone-built homesteads with type 5.

Grasses are almost all perennial throughout the area and constitute 'sour' grazing which loses palatability and nutritional value after early growth from May onwards until the new flush appears the following season; this may be a constraint to pastoralism, especially in the high grasslands where there is little supplement from browse.

It is doubtful if the high grasslands and bracken scrub represent the original vegetation. The climax vegetation here would probably have been evergreen forest of type 1 which was cleared by human action, with the present types maintained by fierce grass fires. The archaeological evidence for occupation of the highlands from around AD 1300 provides the probable agency for this clearance, but there is as yet no positive botanical evidence for it. The regeneration of rain forest over stone structures south-west of Mount Nyangani and also on Chirimanyimo would appear to support this forest climax view, at least under climatic conditions similar to the present.

There is a common belief in some circles that non-indigenous plants were introduced by foreigners seen as responsible for the stone structures, and that they are still associated with the ruins. This goes back at least to Richard Hall in 1909, who attributed several supposed exotic species to Arab influence. Botanists, however, disagree and have specifically refuted that any plants connected with the ruins are not indigenous. Nor is there any evidence whatever that Arabs, Phoenicians or any other exotic peoples ever settled here.

CHAPTER 2
Settlement Sites and the Development of the Complex

The stone builders were not the first inhabitants of the Nyanga region, nor even the first farmers. Surface finds of Early and Middle Stone Age tools dating back to at least two hundred thousand years ago can be found in both the lowlands and highlands, while later Stone Age sites have been investigated by Keith Robinson in the western lowlands. The earliest farmers are represented by Early Iron Age 'Ziwa' pottery dating from about AD 300 to around AD 1000. This was first found by Randall-MacIver in 1905 at the foot of Ziwa mountain, and there are other sites to west and east of the highlands.

It is an unfortunate ambiguity that this name has been applied both to this early pottery and to the Ziwa stone ruins, the latter of later date and quite a different cultural tradition. The Ziwa pottery belongs to the wider Early Iron Age complex of related wares found in much of the southern half of Africa from Lake Victoria to southern Natal and representing the initial spread of Bantu-speaking peoples. In Nyanga the makers of this pottery were certainly farmers with some livestock, and there is some evidence that they may have built crude terraces of granite. There is no resemblance between this pottery and that associated with the later structures, while there may be a time gap of a couple of centuries between them. Thus no continuity can be traced.

Development of the Nyanga complex

The various components of the complex, as outlined in the Preface, can be conveniently divided into the agricultural works and dwelling sites. The agricultural works are described in Chapter 3 and comprise the terraces themselves and the cultivation ridges in the lowlands and valleys, together with the water furrows and other hydraulic works. All of these are difficult to date, except where they are associated with datable settlements. The dwelling sites include homesteads of different designs and apparently defensive structures called 'forts'. There are also iron-working sites which can be considered with the dwelling sites.

The focus of habitation and types of settlements and homesteads have changed through the duration of the complex. These habitation sites can be broadly dated and show shifts in altitudinal zones and changing design. An outline is given here and the stages discussed in more detail below.

The earliest stage identified is represented by a series of quite large sites crowning the highest peaks and ridge tops at around 2,000m or more, along the northern highlands from World's View above Nyanga village to the northern end of the range north of Chirimanyimo Hill. These date from the 14th and 15th centuries and are here referred to as 'early hilltop settlements'. They are succeeded by a slight downwards shift to around 1,800m or 1,900m in broadly the same area, represented by 'ruined pit-structures'. These have been dated to the 16th and

17th centuries. No sites have been identified, or at least dated, in the lowlands contemporary with these stages.

The 17th or early 18th century saw a wider territorial expansion and the development of varying homestead designs. Right through the highlands between 1,400m and about 1,800m above sea level we find the typical well-preserved pit-structures (the 'slave pits' of colonial imagination). At the same time there is occupation of the lowlands. Around the Ziwa area are pit-*enclosures*, closely related to but distinct from the pit-*structures*. To the north from about St Mary's/ Maristvale through Nyautare to Ruangwe, on both sides of the Ruangwe range, are homesteads of a different design called 'double concentric enclosures'. East of the highlands in the Kagore/Regina Coeli area are other enclosures with pits of slightly different design from the Ziwa ones, while in a limited area across the highlands north of Chirimanyimo between Kagore and Nyautare are a number of 'split-level enclosures' of different design again.

The development of the complex may be summarised provisionally as follows:

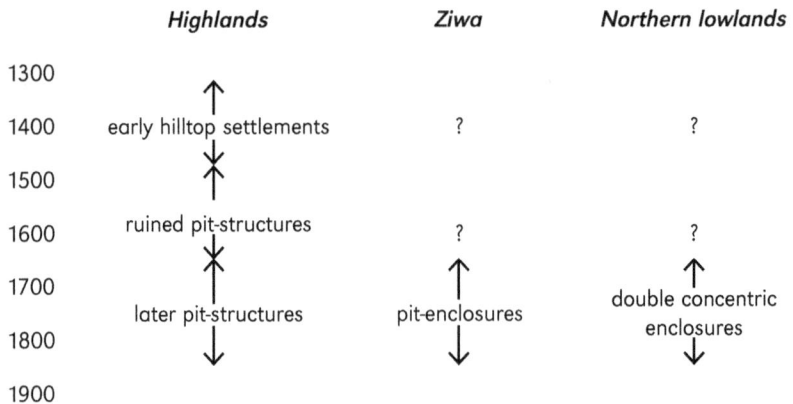

	Highlands	Ziwa	Northern lowlands
1300	↑		
1400	early hilltop settlements	?	?
1500	⚡↑		
1600	ruined pit-structures	?	?
1700	⚡↑	↑	↑
1800	later pit-structures ↓	pit-enclosures ↓	double concentric enclosures ↓
1900			

The precise dating of the later part of the complex is not yet reliably established. Dating by glass beads and pottery is imprecise, and the radiocarbon determinations younger than 450 years ago have alternative calibrations. (Radiocarbon dates are listed in the appendix, with an explanation of their calibration.) The earlier phases also need more radiocarbon determinations for a better definition of their full time-span. The picture may also be incomplete in that other categories of sites may not have been recognised or dated.

The chronology and patterns of distribution of the successive stages may be partly explained by possible changes of climate, which would have affected the viability of occupation and subsistence at different altitudes. Relevant factors would be temperature, rainfall and the wet-season cloud-base. The last of these would have been influential in determining the upper limits of effective settlement because of the dense mist that it occasions in the highlands, sometimes persisting for days at a time; nowadays the critical level is about 1,900m, although some people have recently been attracted above this altitude by the favourable conditions for potato cultivation. The climatic history outlined in Chapter 1 suggested cold and probably dry conditions between AD 1300 and 1500, somewhat warmer/wetter to about 1675, and cooler/drier again to about 1850, followed by amelioration to present conditions. While some climatic motivation for shifts in settlement will be suggested, a solely climatic determination of occupation zones is not entirely convincing, at least on presently available data, although it may have stimulated adaptation in terms of different crops or varieties and the relative importance of livestock. Doubtless, undocumented human political and social factors played an equal or more influential role.

The first two settlement stages are not directly associated with terraces since the sites are all above the upper limit of terracing, which is at around 1,700 m. The higher well-preserved pit-structures are also above the terracing, but lower examples on the escarpments are intimately associated, as are the lowland enclosures. Thus the terracing can be dated at least from the late 17th century and could have started earlier if initiated by the inhabitants of the ruined pit-structures.

Settlements

The different types of settlements and homestead structures belonging to the complex will now be described in more detail. Some typical structures within homesteads – divided houses and raised platforms – are also described, as are iron-working sites. The distribution of most of the different types of settlement structures is more or less mutually exclusive in time and/or space, and they characterise different periods or areas within the complex as outlined above. The site of Mount Muozi is unique and will be described separately, as will three other atypical sites.

Highland settlements

Early hilltop settlements
These are the earliest stone-built sites so far recognised and, as noted above, are found at high elevations between 2,000 m and 2,400 m all along the northern highland range. The lower part of an ash midden on Mount Muozi (see below) belongs with these. They are characterised by small, scattered walled hollows, now usually densely vegetated, among boulder formations, and larger low-walled enclosures on the surrounding open slopes. Terraced house platforms also occur on several sites, such as Chirimanyimo Hill, Muozi and Rukotso. Total site size often reaches 300 m or more in maximum dimension, representing relatively large nucleated villages. They are distinct from the 'forts' described below or the less formal but probably defensive walled hilltops such as Demera Hill above Nyanga town.

Chirimanyimo Hill is the largest and most impressive site, spread over an area 700 m × 500 m on the hilltop and surrounding slopes. The hilltop itself is a fairly level plateau, the eastern half of which is bounded by a stone wall around 1.5 m high. Within this on the western side of the plateau are a number of irregular walled enclosures, within which are traces of house floors, and a walled 'avenue' runs east–west between them to an open area of bare rock, perhaps a meeting place. Below the crest on the steeper and more sheltered western side are a series of terraced platforms, also with remains of house floors, and an enclosure with a more substantial wall entered by a steeply sloping passage from above; this has a floor of uneven bedrock and must have been for livestock. Below this hilltop plateau, especially on a broad shoulder of the hill to the north-east, are numerous low-walled enclosures and walled hollows of the usual type. This site, with its large size and special features on the hilltop plateau, appears more important than the other hilltop settlements and may have been the residence of a chief. There was, however, no evidence of relative material wealth, the only exotic find being a single glass bead.

The low-walled enclosures are around 20 m in diameter and the walls are usually formed by a double line of large vertical stones, originally with an earth-fill between, which probably formed the base of a quickset hedge. These were probably hedged homesteads, but none have been excavated.

The walled hollows are common to all sites. They range in diameter from about three to seven metres and are sunk up to a metre or so below the surrounding surface. In sloping situations the wall may be freestanding on the lower side and more of a revetment – the facing of stonework reinforcing a bank or wall – on the upper side. These were probably for livestock and seem to be a prototype for the pits of the later pit-structures. One excavated example had a floor surfaced with small cobbles and at one side a small grave had been dug through this floor, presumably for the owner (Fig. 4). This measures only 65 cm × 55 cm centimetres and contained a tightly bundled body buried on its back, legs and pelvis uppermost, only 25 cm below floor level. The upper part of the skeleton was cleaned as far as possible and photographed, but left undisturbed. No ornaments or other grave goods were found. After the burial the hollow was abandoned and the walls partly knocked down. It was then used for the disposal of rubbish, represented by thousands of broken potsherds and a few surviving fragments of bone and cattle teeth. Another example was partially excavated at Chirimanyimo Hill within and at one side of a low-walled enclosure. Again the walls had been partly demolished on abandonment and the hollow used for refuse disposal, but no grave was found in the area excavated.

Analysis of the pottery from these sites shows cultural continuity to the early ruined pit-structures of the 16th or 17th century (see below), showing that these settlements belong to the Nyanga complex as a whole.

The hilltop locations lack ready access to surface water in most cases and are ostensibly very exposed. They must have been very cold in winter, the more so as their occupation spanned the first cold phase. However, drier conditions may have raised the cloud-base and reduced the occurrence of unpleasant dense mist, and the hilltops may have attracted more of any available moisture. Exposure to the elements (and to any enemy) might have been mitigated by mountain forest if the highlands were originally forested, as discussed in Chapter 1. The presence of cattle bones at the excavated sites shows that at least some open pasture must have been available. It is likely that shifting cultivation around these settlements involved the clearance of any climax forest, utilising and exhausting its accumulated organic fertility, thus starting the process of conversion to short grassland.

It is uncertain why these high hilltops should have been selected for occupation at this stage. They do not appear to have been prestige sites of a wider society since they lack any evidence of obvious wealth and no contemporary sites of lesser importance have been identified at lower elevations. Relative importance is, however, apparent for Chirimanyimo Hill. The rarity or absence of glass beads or other recognisable imports indicates cultural isolation, and the tightly clustered nucleated settlement pattern contrasts strongly with the much looser dispersed groupings of the ruined and later pit-structures. This could suggest that refuge or concealment from some external threat was involved, although there is no sign of any communal defensive measures and there are no relevant historical records for this period to substantiate or rebut this. A possible threat, direct or indirect, could have been the Great Zimbabwe state which was extending its influence at around this time, as shown by the Harleigh Farm *zimbabwe* near Rusape whose dating is broadly contemporaneous. Threats from the east or north are also possible, but no information is available for these areas.

Fig. 4: Grave cut through the cobbled floor of a walled hollow, Nyangui 1732DD27

Ruined pit-structures

The second stage of settlement is represented by the ruined pit-structures, whose distribution extends from just south of Chirimanyimo Hill down the eastern side of the highland range to Nyanga Downs near Troutbeck. Most are at a higher elevation than the succeeding well-preserved pit-structures. These ruined pits are now seen as broad, grassy hollows, with little visible trace of their original stone lining (Fig. 5). They are situated on sloping ground, and the lower side has been built up to level the surrounding of the pit. There is usually a slight depression in the upper margin, marking the position of an entrance passage, and often another at the lower edge, presumed to be over a drain.

Two sites have been partially excavated, Nyangui G7/1 and Matinha I/1. Both show similar construction: a pit originally 8m to 9m in diameter and 2m or 2.5m deep, paved and revetted with stones, with a sunken entrance passage on the upper side, again stone-paved and revetted (Fig. 6). This passage does not appear to have been roofed, as were the tunnel entrances of the later pit-structures. Above the pit on the upper side are traces of house floors, although these do not have the low stone walls characteristic of the later pits. The stone lining of the pit sides is of rather poor quality, partly accounting for their ruined state.

The G7/1 site is notable for the finds of beads, 119 of glass and 16 of copper; however, only four glass beads and eight of copper were found at Matinha, perhaps suggesting relative wealth. The glass beads are of types dated elsewhere in Zimbabwe to the 16th or 17th century, consistent with the radiocarbon dates. The pottery from both sites is clearly related to that from the early hilltop settlements,

Fig. 5: Grassy hollow of a ruined pit-structure

showing cultural continuity. We may thus infer that the pits are a development from the walled hollows of the earlier sites and that both were used for penning livestock – almost certainly cattle, as argued for the later pit-structures.

The pottery and beads from the upper part of the midden on Mount Muozi (see below) show it to have been occupied at the same time as the ruined pits, although none of these pits occur at Muozi because there was no scope for keeping cattle on the small, isolated plateau. The glass beads here are of identical types and similar frequencies to those from G7/1, and the copper beads are also similar in shape and size although the Muozi ones are of thinner metal. Beads of snail shell and ostrich eggshell were also found at Muozi, where conditions in the midden are favourable for their preservation.

The downward movement from the hilltops to the ruined pit-structures may have coincided with the warmer, wetter intermediate climatic phase when a lower cloud-base may have influenced settlement. However, there is also a marked change in residence pattern from the nucleated villages of the hilltop settlements to loose groupings of individual homesteads representing dispersed villages. This change in residence pattern may imply some relaxation of any constraints affecting the location of earlier settlement and must certainly reflect changes in social organisation.

Well-preserved pit-structures

These are a common feature of the Nyanga terrace complex, found in their hundreds, if not thousands, in the Eastern Highlands from beyond Chirimanyimo

Fig. 6: Pit and entrance passage with stone paving and revetment, Matinha

hill in the north at least as far as the Penhalonga area in the south. They are remarkably standardised in their basic features throughout their distribution (Fig. 7). They take the form of an artificial platform built out from a slope so that the upper edge is at about ground level. The sides and lower edge are revetted with stone facing, the lower edge being commonly 1.5m to 2m high. The platform is roughly oval, 15m to 25m in diameter, and in larger examples often has an irregular plan through the addition of extensions.

Within the platform, more or less central, is a large stone-lined pit, usually 4m to 9m in diameter and 1.8m to 3m deep (Fig. 8). The base of this pit, if not on bedrock, is paved with flat stones. The walls of the pit would have been built up as the platform was constructed. They are neatly built of irregular-shaped stones cunningly fitted and wedged to form a vertical face. The largest stones were reserved for the coping around the top and may measure up to a metre or more in length and 40cm in height, weighing several hundred kilograms. No evidence of roofing has ever been noticed. In rare cases there may be two pits within the same platform.

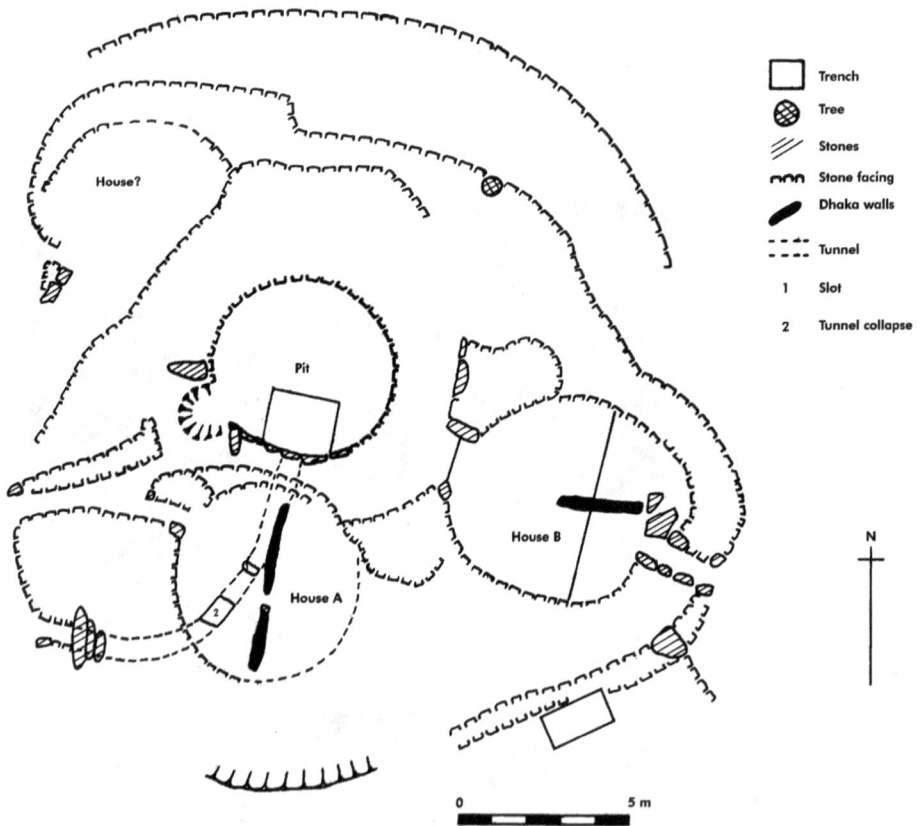

Fig. 7: Plan of pit-structure, National Park

Access to the pit is through a curved tunnel from the upper side (Fig. 3). Tunnels are neatly walled, and roofed and paved with flat slabs. Entrances at either end have remarkably consistent measurements: 1.1 m high and 50 cm wide with a variation of about 10 cm. The length of the tunnel varies but is commonly around seven metres. The exterior entrance usually has an open revetted passage sloping down from ground level. At the lower side of the pit is a small sump to a drain about 20 cm high and 25 cm wide which leads through the platform to emerge on the slope below or into a sunken ditch if the base of the pit is well below ground level.

In a fair number of cases a radial wall extends outwards from the platform up to 25 m or more, roughly on the contour and often curving uphill; this is interpreted as sheltering a homestead garden. Some also have small basins around 3 m wide, dammed by a stone wall immediately below the drain outlet from the pit, while others have ditches leading to a small hollow below; these would impound effluent draining from the pit.

On the platform around the pit are walled bays for houses or other structures, the rough stone walls being about 50 cm high. The majority of such bays are between four and five metres in diameter, but they may be as little as two or as much as seven metres. One house, usually the largest, is invariably sited above the tunnel and has a slot near the middle of the floor through which logs could have been dropped vertically to close the tunnel. Up to eight other house-bays may be

Fig. 8: Pit-structure with restored houses, National Park

arranged on the platform around the pit, and a narrow walkway may be left most of the way around the edge. Within the walled bays, house walls were constructed of close-set poles plastered with *dhaka* (clay) on the inside. Adjacent to the house over the tunnel there is often a smaller bay with a higher floor; excavation of one example showed a floor laid on stone slabs with a cavity beneath, and this was probably some kind of storage hut. Some pit-structures have the normal type of raised platforms for storage huts, as described below for the lowland enclosures.

Many of the houses are divided by a low cross-wall from 15 cm to 50 cm high (Fig. 9). One half has a plastered clay floor with a central hearth, a grinding stone set in the floor, and often small compartments formed by moulded *dhaka* kerbs. The other half, usually at a lower level, is roughly paved with stones. There are separate entrances to each half of the house, one from outside the platform to the paved half and the other from the floored side to the pit surround. Such divided houses are found throughout the distribution of the highland pit-structures, and identical houses occur in the lowland pit-enclosures of the Ziwa area described below. They are not, however, found in the double concentric enclosures of the northern lowlands.

The plastered rooms were clearly kitchens for the processing and preparation of food, and doubtless were used for other domestic activities. The lower rooms with their rough paved floors and separate entrances must have been for the penning of small stock such as goats at night. Such stock could perhaps have been the personal property of the wife whose kitchen it was. Several such houses in a homestead may imply a polygamous household. Surviving memories of traditional kitchens of the Nyama people document this type of divided house and the keeping of goats within it.

The function of the pit as accommodation for small cattle is recounted in a number of other recorded traditions but most observers have been reluctant to accept it because they could not conceive of cattle small enough to enter the tunnels. However, the Muozi site has now provided bones of dwarf cattle only a metre or so in height, which may have been a special breed. Dwarf cattle are known from other parts of Africa (Selous saw them in Zambia) and there are oral traditions about them in Zimbabwe. The central defended situation within the heart of the homestead indicates that cattle were valuable property. A number of pits have been excavated or cleared out over the last century, and no original deposits have been found beyond some silting and the accumulation of leaf-mould after abandonment. They must therefore have been regularly cleaned out during use but, as no resulting heaps of dung have been found, this must have been taken for manuring the gardens or fields (see Chapter 4). Some manure could also have been dried and used as fuel if firewood was in short supply.

The pit-structures were residential units for families and their stock, with the cattle stalled in the pit where they would have been sheltered from the cold winds of winter and protected from surreptitious theft; goats and sheep and probably calves were kept within the houses. They thus represent the family homesteads of the general population. They are often loosely clustered in the landscape in groups of anything up to thirty within an area of up to ten hectares. In some cases

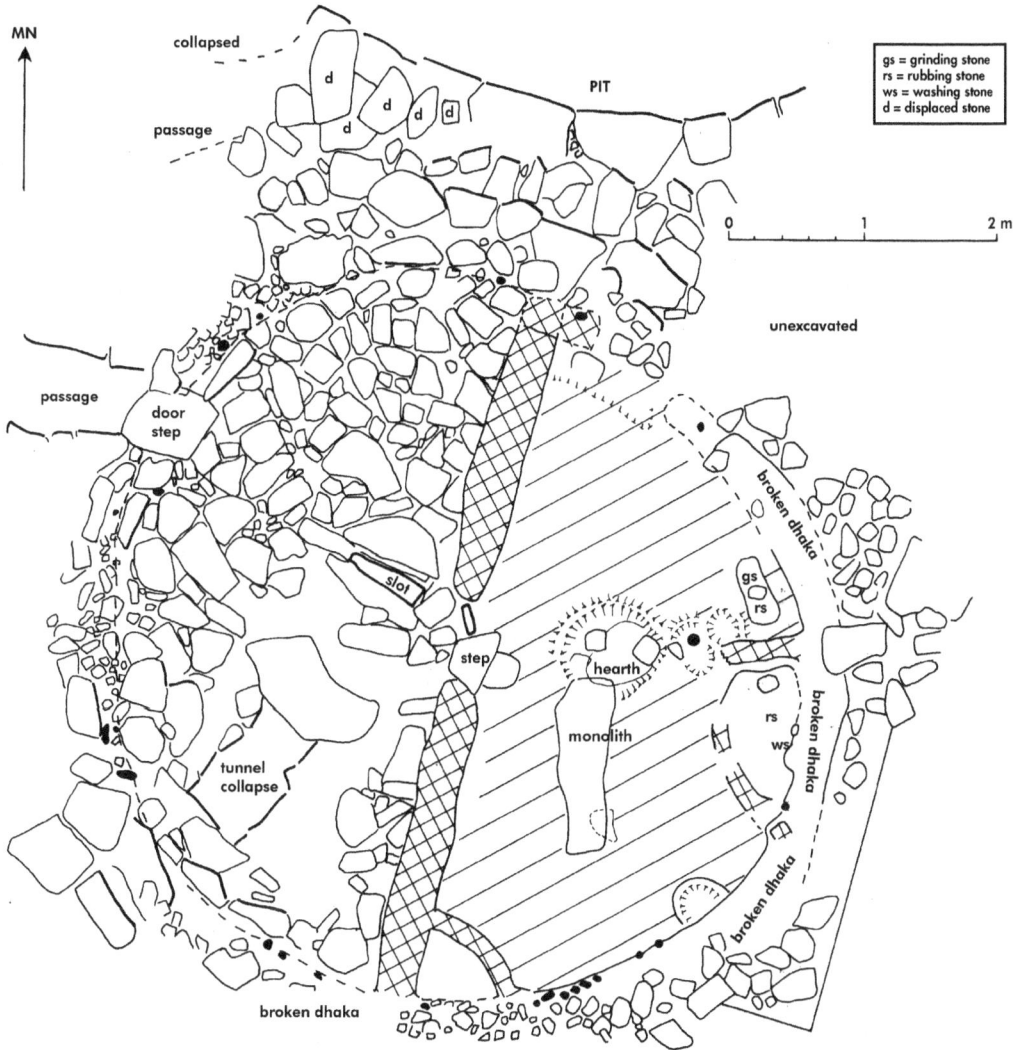

Fig. 9: Plan of a divided house, National Park

such groups or individual examples were served by artificial water furrows, as noted in the next chapter. Water from these could have been led through the pits themselves and there are occasional traces of channels for this. The impoundment of slurry effluent from the pits has also been mentioned and is discussed further in Chapter 4.

These pit-structures appear to date from the 18th to mid-19th centuries. Those on Rhodes Estate (now Nyanga National Park), some of the best preserved, had been abandoned some time before the 1890s, but probably not very long before on the evidence of well-preserved *dhaka* features and three recent radiocarbon determinations (see Appendix; the 17th century date from Fishpit is not consistent with the well-preserved *dhaka* structure with which it is associated and must be anomalous). Glass beads found in excavations, though generally few, are of types also consistent with this time range.

The interpretation of the pits as cattle pens in the centre of the homestead indicates the increasing importance of cattle, materially and doubtless ideologically. It also implies adequate pasture, showing that the highlands cannot all have been densely forested by this time. Pit diameters for well-preserved examples range between 3.5m and 11m. While there is considerable variation in size at all altitudes, the average diameter shows a clear increase above 1,800m, indicating the greater importance of cattle above the upper limit of terracing. The association of terracing with the lower well-preserved pit-structures shows the parallel importance of cultivation.

These features have fascinated observers over the past century, and earlier explanations for the pits, reasoned or fanciful, may be of some interest to the curious. Most observers were reluctant to accept the cattle explanation in spite of oral traditions to that effect. Early writers saw them as dungeons for slaves employed in building and working the terraces, and the term 'slave pits' is still current in some circles. Other improbable explanations have been mine shafts and gold-washing tanks; refuges for women and children in time of danger; defensive bunkers; water-storage tanks; grain silos as a symbolic representation of Astarte's womb; or (tongue-in-cheek) as play-pens for keeping the children out of mischief while their mothers were busy.

Split-level enclosures

This type of homestead appears to be restricted to an area across the highland ridge north of Chirimanyimo hill between the foot of the western and eastern escarpments, with an altitudinal range of 1,290m to 1,700m.

They are oval to circular in plan, built on sloping ground, with a relatively massive outer wall up to about 1.8m high. The design varies to some extent but has common features. Within the outer wall on the lower side is an oval, pit-like chamber, its upper side deeply revetted. This chamber is in most cases subdivided by internal walls or lines of vertical slabs and is entered from above by a short, steeply ramped passage. At different levels above it are house-bays, and the single main entrance is a tunnel-like passage through the outer wall to one such bay, from the side rather than from above. Internal size ranges from 8m × 8m to 20m × 17m and the number of house-bays from one to four. Several have small 'cupboards' built into the walls of house-bays or lower chambers, a feature quite common at the site of Chirangeni (see below) but rare elsewhere. The lower chamber may be paved with stones and must have been for livestock, perhaps cattle, calves and small stock, segregated by the dividing walls. These must have entered through one of the houses. Dating is unknown; there is no impression of any great age and they could post-date or be contemporary with neighbouring pit-structures.

Lowland enclosures

Lowland enclosures have been classified into a number of consistent forms: simple enclosures, pit-enclosures, and double concentric enclosures. All represent homesteads, and terraces often directly abut the walls or are closely adjacent. Homestead location avoids the valleys and may be on relatively gentle slopes or level ground; all are found below an altitude of 1,400m. The distribution of the latter two types is mutually exclusive, pit-enclosures at and around Ziwa and double concentric to the north, from St Mary's through Nyautare to Ruangwe. Both probably extend west across the Nyangombe river. Both types are similar in size and basic plan, with the well-built central pit or small enclosure interpreted as a cattle pen. However, the double concentric enclosures lack lintelled entrances and divided houses, and their outer walls are generally low, often with multiple entrances. Related simple enclosures in both areas lack the central pit or enclosure.

In most lowland areas there are also occurrences of stone walls with no consistent configuration; these are probably also occupation sites, but no description or classification has been attempted. In addition there are small enclosures four metres or less in internal diameter, probably individual houses, which occur singly or in small groups unassociated with a larger enclosure; these are especially common in the Maristvale/St Mary's area.

The pit-enclosures date from the 18th to early 19th centuries, although a greater spread is not ruled out. Their form indicates a development from the well-preserved pit-structures with which they are at least partly contemporary. The northern enclosures, including the double concentric type, also appear to continue well into the 19th century, but their beginning is uncertain.

Pit-enclosures

These are distinct from the highland pit-*structures*, although there are close affinities between the two types (Fig. 10). They are usually built on a gentle slope, from which an artificial revetted platform is built out as in the highland pit-structures, but here of lesser height, rarely more than a metre or a metre and a half. The entrance is on the upper side, where the wall is around 1.2m high and usually greatly thickened, thicknesses of up to four metres being not uncommon. The entrance thus takes the form of a narrow passage, often roofed with stone slabs, with dimensions comparable to those of the pit-structure tunnels, around 1.1m high and 50cm wide. In many cases there are sockets in the sides of the passage for a wooden drawbar, which must have been built into the wall. The circumference is often interrupted by houses or raised platforms whose *dhaka* walls would have completed the enclosure perimeter. Fragments of baked *dhaka* with pole- and stick-impressions are often found on the wall.

The platform accommodates a more or less central stone-lined pit, usually 2.5m to 3.5m in diameter and around 1.5m deep, the floor paved if not on bedrock. Access to this is by a sunken passage, again often lintelled, starting from just inside the main enclosure entrance; this may also have drawbar sockets. In a high proportion of cases the passage has been deliberately blocked at one end or sometimes completely filled with stones, apparently when the homestead was abandoned. There is always a drain at the lower side of the pit leading out through the platform. Around the pit there may be raised platforms and house floors (often of the divided type described above). As with the pit-structures, it is deduced that the pit in each enclosure would have housed a few dwarf cattle, while the divided houses included provision for small stock. There are often several divided houses in an enclosure, suggesting a polygamous family with a kitchen for each wife.

Raised platforms are a typical feature of lowland enclosures in all areas, and they also occur, though less regularly, in highland pit-structures. These have a floor of stone slabs around three metres in diameter, usually capped with *dhaka*, raised from the ground on vertical stones. They would have had *dhaka* walls and a thatched roof and are usually interpreted as storage granaries by comparison with such structures still in use in the area, which, however, are rectangular since the platform is made of logs. The raised floors provide ventilation beneath and some protection from termites. Some of the larger examples may have been sleeping huts.

Many enclosures, both with and without pits (simple enclosures), are linked by stone-walled pathways to longer arterial walled passages leading through the terraced fields.

An interesting item associated with one of the largest pit-enclosures at Ziwa is

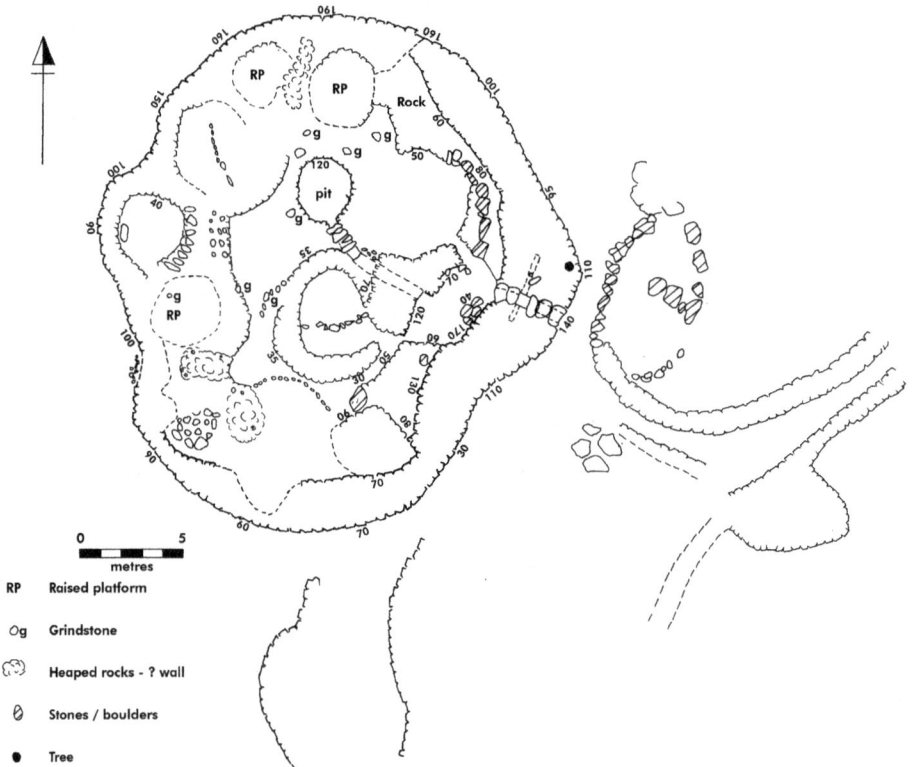

RP   Raised platform

Og   Grindstone

        Heaped rocks - ? wall

        Stones / boulders

●   Tree

Fig. 10: Plan of a pit-enclosure, Ziwa

a 'rock gong' (Fig. 11). This is a slab of dolerite about 1.25m long and 6cm to 20cm thick, propped up on other stones in such a way that it can vibrate and produce a clear bell-like note when struck with a stone. The lower, thinner edge is smoothed from constant hammering. Here the gong doubtless signifies the importance of this enclosure, perhaps the residence of a local headman or ritual specialist.

Double concentric enclosures

In the northern lowlands, the double concentric enclosures appear to be the equivalent of the Ziwa pit-enclosures. These structures have an outer wall, often low and roughly built, with one or more plain entrances and a more solid inner enclosure. The inner enclosure is well built, the wall around 1.2m high and about a metre thick, with a plain entrance and internal diameter ranging from two to five metres. There may be a drain on the lower side.

Such enclosures are often built on level ground, but some built on slopes have the interior divided by a terrace. There may be houses or raised platforms between the inner and outer walls, but typical divided houses do not seem to occur in this area. One example in the Chigura hills (Fig. 12) is appended to a residential simple enclosure with houses, raised platforms and grinding stones. Several of the houses had internal raised platforms and must have been primarily for storage. This site must represent the homestead of a relatively wealthy family, with three households/kitchens and four storage houses. Livestock would have been housed in the adjacent double concentric enclosure, probably a few cattle in the central enclosure and possibly small stock in the outer. There seems to be no special provision for small stock in the houses. The double enclosure had apparently been deliberately blocked. The homestead was destroyed by fire at, or perhaps after, its abandonment.

Fig. 11: Rock gong at Ziwa

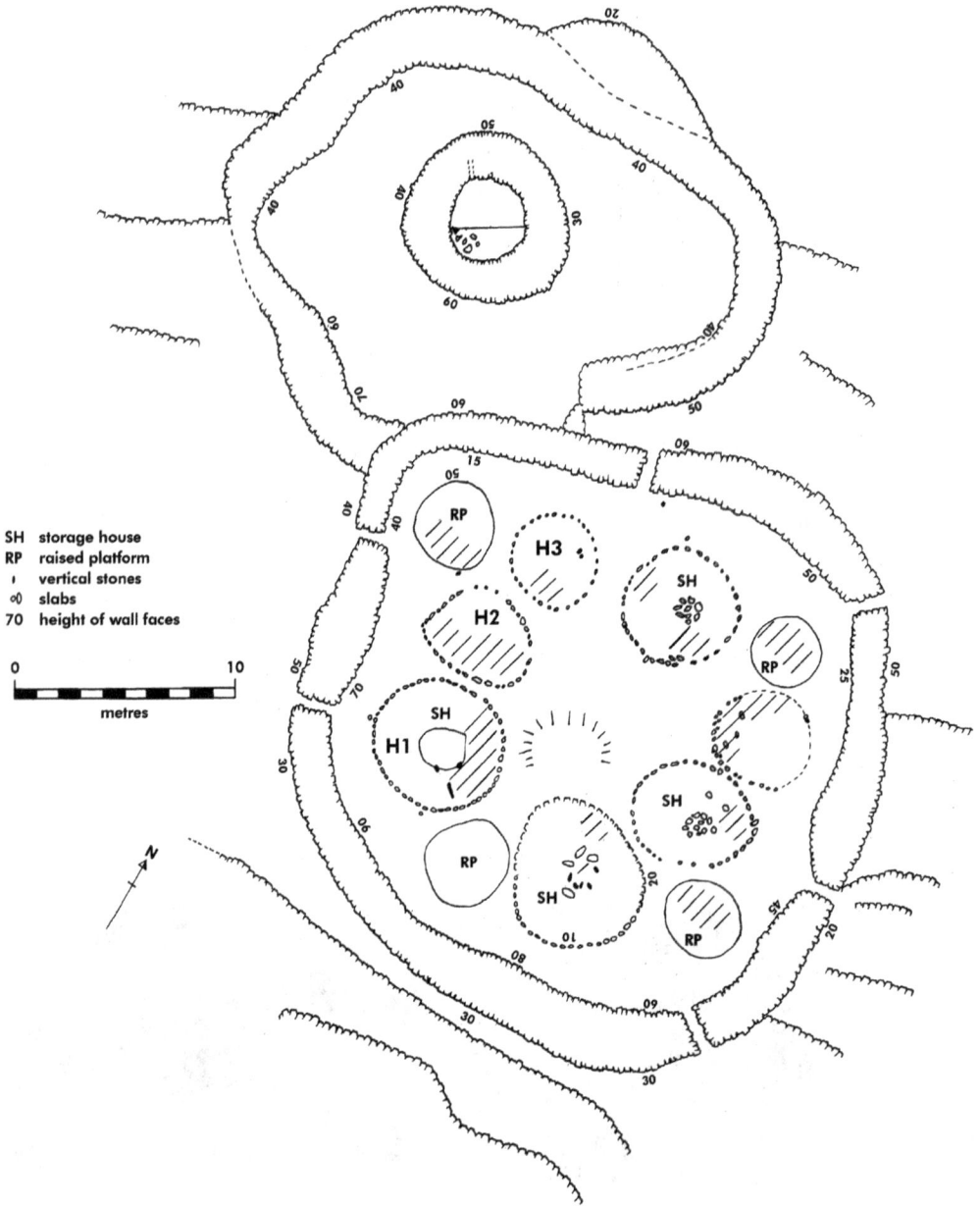

SH storage house
RP raised platform
ı   vertical stones
∞   slabs
70 height of wall faces

Fig. 12: Plan of a double concentric enclosure appended to a residential enclosure, Chigura

Other sites

There are a number of sites, some relatively large, which do not fit neatly into any of the above standardised categories. Of these, Mount Muozi and Chirangeni have been most fully investigated.

Muozi

Muozi is unique among known sites of the Nyanga complex in that it appears to have been occupied throughout most, if not all, of the span of the complex. There is also a substantial ash midden, a feature not observed at any other site. It lies on the summit of Mount Muozi (Fig. 13). This prominent summit, at an altitude of 2,100m, forms a small, isolated plateau surrounded on three sides by precipitous cliffs, at the end of a long spur projecting from the main western escarpment of the highlands above Maristvale Mission and Nyanga High School.

The plateau is about 275m long × 120m wide, and a further promontory projects from the south-west corner. Much of the plateau has evidence of occupation, including some walled hollows, and there are stone walls and house floors on the promontory. There are house platforms and much broken pottery on the very steep approach from the neck of the spur, on which are a number of conical stone cairns.

The ash midden is at the western edge of the main plateau just above the top of the western cliff and measures about 14m long, 7m wide and up to 1.4m deep. It contains much pottery, beads of glass and copper and well-preserved bone fragments and shell beads. Five human hand and foot bones suggest that the excavated trench may have cut the edge of a grave, undetected in the homogeneous deposits. The lower part of the deposits is firmly dated by radiocarbon to the early 15th century, contemporary with the early hilltop settlements. The middle to upper deposits appear to date between the early 16th and early 17th centuries, thus contemporary with the ruined pit-structures. The top of the sequence may be mid-17th or even late 18th century.

The accumulation of this large midden, the only such feature found on any of the Nyanga sites, may perhaps be explained by the limitations of the plateau situation, which allowed little scope for cultivation and the attendant use of domestic ash and rubbish for manure, and by the difficulties of transporting this material to terraced fields which must have been on the escarpment at some distance.

The bones from the midden provide the only relatively large and well-preserved collection from Nyanga. Most represent domesticated animals, mainly cattle with some goats and sheep, and there are a few traces of chicken, dog and house rat. Bones of wild animals are rare. Cattle leg bones are of a dwarf variety with an average shoulder height of around one metre. Thus there were cattle in Nyanga from at least the 15th century which would have been small enough to pass through the restricted tunnels and entrance passages of the pit-structures and enclosures. This strongly supports the function of the pits as cattle pens, even though there are no such pits on the Muozi site itself.

Fig. 13: Mount Muozi from the east side of the saddle

The stone ruins on the promontory (Fig. 14) are later in date than the ash midden and most of the remains on the plateau: a date in the 18th or early 19th century may be suggested. At the south-western corner of the plateau a sunken pathway leads into a large hollow with revetted walls, 20 m long, 9 m wide and around 1.5 m deep, with a second hollow adjoining it. From the southern corner of the first hollow a path leads down to the neck or saddle of the promontory that juts out to the west. This neck is divided by a low east–west wall and the whole southern edge of the promontory is revetted by a retaining wall along the top of the steep slope. On the south side of the saddle are three low house platforms, one of which has a collection of seventeen complete and partly broken pots (Fig. 15), ranging from small bowls to large, wide-mouthed pots up to more than 60 cm in diameter and height, with a capacity of up to 140 litres. There are at least fifteen other more or less complete pots among the stone ruins. Several of these pots are of types unique to this site; a few are of types found in the highland pit-structures, while others are more typical of the lowland enclosures.

To the north-west of these house platforms is a high platform, partly formed by a natural rock and partly revetted to a height of at least 80 cm. At least ten long thin stones up to 80 cm long have fallen radially from this and seem originally to have stood on top, where a few slabs may have been part of a decking. Below this platform is a large, flat-topped rectangular rock which, to the imaginative, might conjure ideas of an altar. An entrance passes to the west of the platform.

The steep slope on the north side of the saddle is a soft, ashy scree littered with animal bones, including complete horn cores of cattle. A passage leads up behind the high platform to the main enclosure of the complex. It opens into a semicircular courtyard neatly paved with flat stones, on the left of which is a high stone plinth joined to the wall from which numerous grinding stones are spilling.

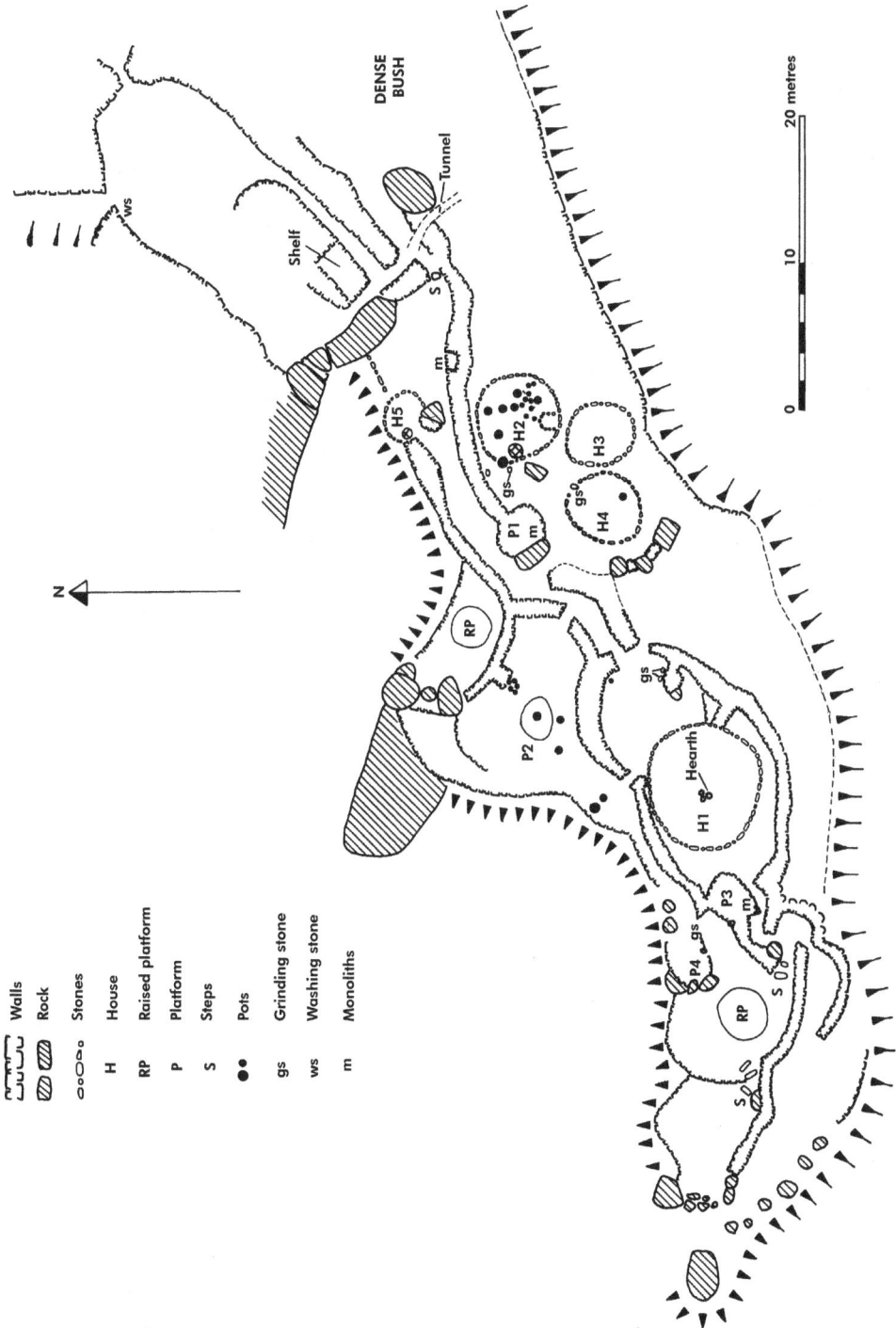

Fig. 14: Muozi. Plan of the stone ruins on the western promontory

Fig. 15: Muozi. House circles with the main group of complete pots

The walls here are the best built on the site, about 1.5 m high. To the north is a broad terrace on which is a solid circular platform on top of which is a pot, and eight other vessels of various shapes and sizes are scattered around. A lower terrace to the north-east has a typical raised platform.

In the main enclosure, most of the space behind the court is occupied by a large house some eight metres in diameter. Beyond this house a narrow passage leads out of the enclosure past a solid platform on which is a group of small monoliths, a long, barbed iron spearhead and a unique iron object consisting of four splayed iron strips bound in the middle with a spirally wound bar (Fig. 16). The passage twists down to a terrace walled on the south side, on which is another raised platform three metres in diameter. Steps lead down from here to a final small terrace, also walled on the south side, and beyond are rocks to the tip of the promontory.

Access to the whole promontory complex is restricted to the single passage from the first hollow. Access is further constricted to the main enclosure and large house, presumably that of the principal resident of the site. The solid platforms indicate ritual functions – at the mouth of the path to the main enclosure, on the northern terrace, the high platform beside the passage, the grinding stone plinth in the courtyard, and beyond the main house. The small terraces at the end would appear to be the principal resident's private preserve, with his granary on the raised platform.

This part of the site, and by extension the whole mountain, is of sacred significance to the indigenous Nyama people of the surrounding district. The stone

Fig. 16: Iron object from Muozi

ruins are traditionally associated with a powerful figure among the Nyama people named Muozi, who lived here as a diviner and rain-maker. His riches, fame and popularity were not welcomed by others, including the Saunyama chiefs, and one of these is said to have organised an army to destroy him. His death brought a curse on the Unyama territory so that the rains failed for many consecutive years, until Saunyama decided to pay compensation to appease his avenging spirit. *Rapoko* (finger millet) and beer were, and perhaps still are, sent up the mountain by the hands of members of a clan that had good relations with Muozi. Failure to do this would cause drought and other disasters, and many Nyama people are afraid to climb the mountain to this day.

Other traditions – with a rather conflicting message – say that all Saunyama chiefs used to be installed and buried on Muozi. Traditional procedures and rituals were laid down to be performed before they could approach the site. Some of these procedures have now been discontinued or forgotten, and the last installation is said to have been in 1953. The reuse of the site and restoration of its traditional significance are now under consideration. Out of respect for this sacred aspect, no excavation has been undertaken on the promontory and the pots have been photographed but not disturbed.

Throughout the occupation of the site, the main animal herds must have been kept elsewhere, since grazing and water would have been very limited on the plateau. The main crops also must have been grown at a distance, perhaps on the stone terraces on the escarpment below. Water would have been a problem in the dry season. The nearest accessible water is probably 1,500m distant on the northern side of the main spur where a stream descends from the highlands and there are traces of a path from the base of the saddle in this direction.

Clearly the stone ruins on the promontory, situated in an easily defensible and symbolically prominent position, were the residence of an important person, as recounted in the tradition recorded above. The bone remains on the ashy scree slope indicate fairly lavish meat consumption at this time, both of cattle and smaller animals. The completeness of the pots and the generally fair state of the stone walls would suggest a relatively recent date, though the inaccessibility and sacred nature of the site would discourage much human disturbance.

Chirangeni

The Chirangeni site lies at the foot of the western escarpment, some six kilometres north-east of Nyautare business centre. An area here was selected for a detailed survey of granite terracing, as described in Chapter 3, and included within it is a large enclosure of unique type. After the survey had been carried out, this very area was recognised as having been illustrated in Roger Summers's Nyanga volume in 1958 in an aerial photograph captioned 'Typical area of Lowland Ruins' – a startling coincidence that we should have arrived by different routes at the same few hectares out of the vast area of lowland terracing.

The enclosure is on a slight shoulder of a broad spur at an altitude of 1,350 m, about 70 m above the base of the escarpment. A walled passageway crosses a shallow valley from the north, curves up past the north-eastern side of the enclosure, and continues east up the slope to a small plateau above. Terraces abut the south side of the enclosure and both sides of the passageway and continue below the enclosure. Immediately below the enclosure to the north-west is what appears to be a walled and terraced garden, described with the terracing in the next chapter.

The enclosure (Fig. 17) and houses within it are different in character from any others yet recorded. The enclosure is heart-shaped, measuring 28m × 34m internally, with a vertical fall of 6.6m from south-east to north-west. The outer wall is up to 2.5m wide and 2m high on the lower side but only 70cm high at the upper side. The only entrance is a lintelled passage 1.25m high and 50cm wide on the north-east side, the wall here being 2m thick and 1.8m high.

Within the enclosure are six stone-walled houses, with well-built walls around 1m high and thick. Doorways are plain with no lintels. All have internal divisions formed by lines of vertical slabs and a small *dhaka* hearth. Each has a 'cupboard' for storage built into the thickness of the wall. The walls contrast with the rough, low walls surrounding and reinforcing thin walls of pole and *dhaka* which are the norm at other sites. The wall of the central house incorporates large lumps of baked *dhaka*, indicating a previous *dhaka* structure, perhaps a house which the stone walling has replaced.

The largest house, in the centre of the enclosure, is 4.5m in diameter. At the back a narrow stepped passage with two lintel stones leads down to a smaller second enclosure paved with stones, with a fairly massive wall up to 2m thick and 1.9m high, through which is a drain on the lower side. It thus resembles the pit of a highland pit-structure or a lowland pit-enclosure, but with walls built up from ground level. One half of the main house was a kitchen and living area, with hearth, storage-cupboard and grinding facilities. The other half was paved with stones and would have been for small stock as with the divided houses; it also provided access to the lower enclosure, which, with its resemblance to true pits elsewhere, would have accommodated a few small cattle. There is no other obvious accommodation for cattle within the whole enclosure or, indeed, outside it.

Excavation of a second house immediately to the north shows similar features to the central house but without the attached subsidiary enclosure. One half is again stone-paved, the other half having a rough, clay floor with hearth, grinding stone and cupboard.

Also within the enclosure are two smaller, rougher circular structures, the remains of four raised platforms, two possible floors of houses without stone walls, several large standing stones and a 'balcony' at the highest point on the eastern side

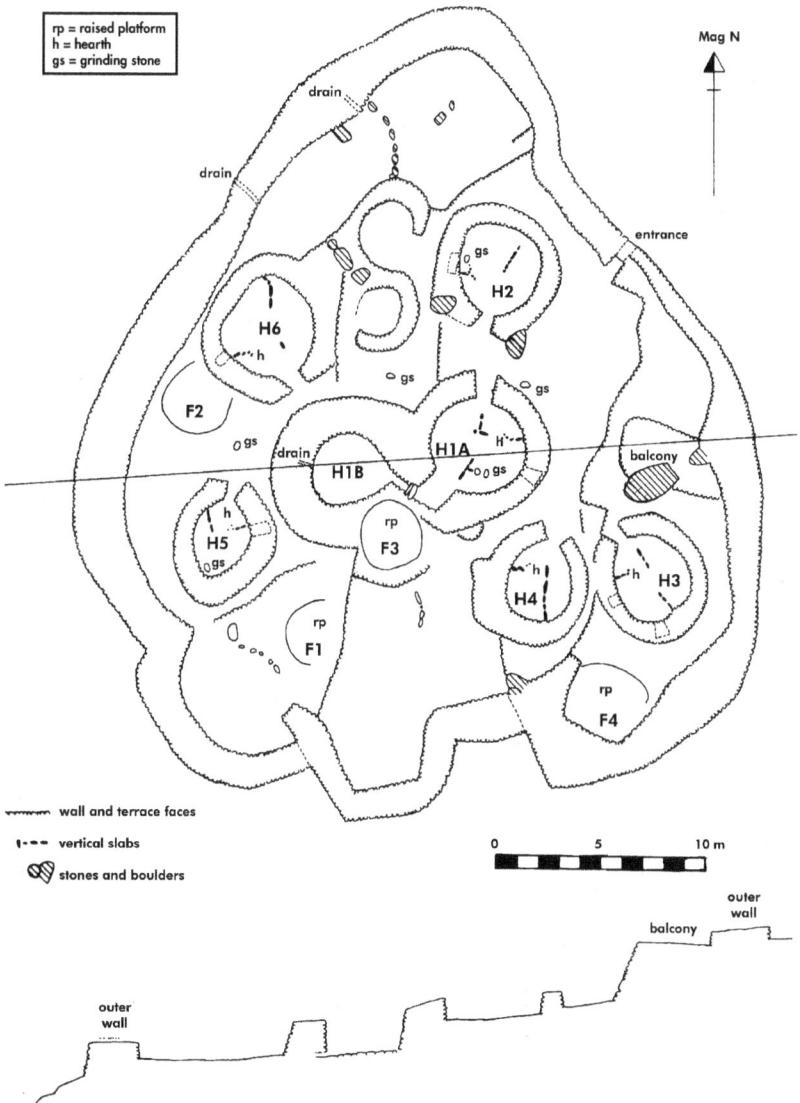

Fig. 17: Chirangeni. Plan of the enclosure

overlooking the whole enclosure. The raised platforms represent storage huts, each associated with a house.

The state of preservation of the enclosure and houses suggests a relatively recent date, probably 19th century, with which one recent radiocarbon date would be consistent. That the site must pre-date AD 1900 is borne out by Carl Peters (1902), who must have passed fairly close by in 1901 and found the whole area depopulated. He was told by a guide from Katerere: 'Men are afraid to dwell here, even to wander alone through this land: it is the country of death.' This must reflect a vivid memory of the struggle between the rival dynastic houses for the Saunyama chiefship in the 19th century.

This enclosure differs from others in the area – and, indeed, in the complex as a whole – as far as present knowledge goes. The size and quality of the outer wall and the lintelled entrance set it apart from normal homesteads in the northern lowlands, which are typically double concentric or simple enclosures with lower walls and house floors. These characteristics show some affinities with 'forts' described below, examples of which occur to the west and south-west, but there are no loopholes and only slight traces of a parapet at the entrance, while the wall on the upper side is hardly high enough to be defensive. The configuration of the central double feature has no known exact parallels. Some of the forts in the National Park do have stone-walled houses within them, sometimes tightly packed, but their walls are lower and more roughly built. The cupboards are a rare feature facilitated by the neat construction of the walls. The internal division of the houses by vertical slabs has some functional parallel to the divided houses of the pit-structures and Ziwa enclosures but is different in detail, while this type of small hearth has also not been noted elsewhere. Other features such as the raised platforms are more typical of the Nyanga complex.

The size and quality of the structures, the number of houses and the extent of the associated terracing and walled garden suggest a locally important social unit, perhaps that of a chief or headman, although the rarity of exotic items such as beads indicates no great relative wealth. The head of the unit is likely to have occupied the central house, with his cattle closely protected in the attached enclosure. Five other households of lesser but approximately equal status occupied the other houses. Small stock of individual households were probably kept within the houses. Manure from livestock and domestic rubbish was almost certainly used in the walled garden and perhaps on the terraced fields. The walled passage provided access to neighbours to the north and to the plateau above and would have kept people and livestock off the fields.

Haro

This is an extensive complex of walls stretching for about 400m along and below the lip of the western escarpment at the head of the Kumbu valley, 2,300m north-north-west of Chirimanyimo Hill. Width down the slope is about 30m to 100m. The walls are rather roughly built and often tumbled and form a series of interlinked irregular enclosures up to about 15m across, with some roughly terraced platforms and smaller enclosures among them. They form a continuous irregular wall along the crest of the slope, with a couple of enclosures extending on to the plateau above. There are at least two concentrations of slag, one associated with baked *dhaka*, but very few potsherds. The age and associations of this site are unknown.

Demera Hill

This site is on top of the large hill east of Nyanga town. A few linear walls appear to divide the space between the twin peaks and there is a wall about 50m long above a steep rock face east of the northern peak. There are a few enclosures and revetted occupation platforms, with a scatter of small potsherds and at least one localised occurrence of slag. The maximum dimension of the site is about 150m. This is not a typical fort nor does it resemble the early hilltop settlements. It can probably be attributed to the Manyika in the 19th or perhaps 18th century.

Homesteads and symbolism

As noted in Chapter 1, the Nyanga stone structures have been characterised as practical 'folk architecture' serving the everyday needs of ordinary people. However, there are aspects of the design of many homesteads that appear to go beyond the requirements of functional efficiency so that an important symbolic element among these everyday needs can be deduced. The only earlier writer to appreciate this element has been Bruwer in 1965, albeit misled by his Phoenician preconceptions in interpreting the pits as symbolic representations of the goddess Astarte's womb. Single standing stones, monoliths, associated with homesteads or in isolated situations have also been conjectured to have had symbolic significance.

The highland pit-structures represent a massive investment of labour in the construction of the platform necessary to accommodate the central pit, and thus the pit itself and the cattle within it assume a central ideological importance. However, there are certain practical advantages. The depth of the pit provides shelter from the winter winds and its position enhances the security of the cattle. While the construction of the tunnel may be seen as over-elaborate, it is an effective solution to the problem of access to attain the requisite depth, built to the minimum dimensions to admit dwarf cattle and supporting a house above to control access and security. The curvature from one side reduces the steepness incurred in a direct approach from above, but the fact that almost all the tunnels curve left into the pit appears to be significant. These tunnels were rarely deliberately blocked, in contrast to the frequent blocking of pit entrance passages in the pit-enclosures at Ziwa.

The ruined pit-structures provide less well-preserved data for speculation. The basic pit is present but probably had an open entrance passage, and the platform is less developed as the focus of settlement around it. Possibly the pit was still primarily functional and had not yet achieved all its symbolic connotations.

The lowland pit-enclosures of the Ziwa area show marked affinities to the pit-structures, such as the presence of the pit and the identical divided houses. However, there are also consistent differences, some of which are also seen in the Ziwa enclosures without pits, and these differences often reflect less functional efficiency. Shelter from the wind cannot have been an important consideration in the warmer conditions of the lowlands and the pits are smaller and shallower. The pit again places the cattle below the level of the houses, but the function of penning livestock could have been more economically accomplished by building a small walled enclosure, as in the double concentric enclosures further north. As it is, the pit entails the massive effort of platform construction for little practical advantage and must reflect the same principles as the highland pits but divorced from their functional qualities, reinforcing the symbolic significance of both.

Again it is hard to see any practical purpose for the lintelled passage entrance to most of the pits, for which an open passage could serve since no great depth is required. The entry to this passage from within the main enclosure entrance differs from the pit-structures but provides more security. The frequent deliberate blocking of many of the pit entrance passages at Ziwa (38 out of a sample of 53) has been mentioned above. This could have had a practical purpose reflecting changing circumstances during occupation of the homestead, but is often in excess of a simple blocking wall so that a symbolic purpose may be more likely.

The entrances to most enclosures at Ziwa, both with and without pits, take the form of a lintelled passage, usually with provision for a wooden drawbar. The wall around the entrance is normally greatly thickened up to four metres, apparently for the express purpose of lengthening the passage and again involving far more effort than is consistent with a simple barrier. The wall is no higher than the lintel stones and little extra security is provided by the latter apart from constraining the entrant to a stooping and more vulnerable posture. There must be strong symbolism in the entry to the homestead through a restricted passage of significant length.

One may conclude that most of the Ziwa residents had surplus resources of labour beyond that required for subsistence, which afforded the luxury of indulging in expensive symbolism in their homesteads.

The double concentric enclosures of the northern lowlands appear more pragmatic in design. The solidly constructed inner enclosure is of the same dimensions as the Ziwa pits but built up from the ground, eliminating the need for a platform. The outer wall of these enclosures is usually lower and often has multiple entrances, while lintelled doorways rarely occur in homesteads, being restricted to forts. These structures are thus more consistent with the economical application of labour to functional needs. The northern lowlands could have been more constrained by economic factors with fewer resources to spare, or may have directed their symbolic proclivities to less tangible or lasting effect.

The split-level enclosures of the northern highlands also seem to involve effort beyond the purely practical but expressed in rather different ways and avoiding the major investment of a full platform. The lower chamber, presumably for livestock, is formed by the high lower wall of the enclosure and entered from within it by a short, open sloping passage. The wall at the entrance, however, is thickened and the entrance passage lintelled as at Ziwa. The passage opens into a house-bay and the cattle and other stock must have passed through this house, as with the central house at Chirangeni.

While an important symbolic factor has been deduced, interpretation of this can be little more than speculation. The features identified as requiring explanation beyond the purely functional concern mainly the pits and tunnels/passages. Among other approaches, sexual symbolism and fertility and the symbolism of transition associated with entrances might provide general analogies, but specific meanings can hardly be reliably inferred.

Forts

These structures vary in size, design and probably in purpose, but have common features indicating a defensive function. They are usually on hilltops or prominent positions and are characterised by relatively massive walls around two metres in height and often two metres thick, forming a complete circuit, except in some cases where they crown a precipitous cliff and that side has been left unguarded. Walls often have a raised parapet on the outer side and a ledge (banquette) on the inner side. Most have 'loopholes' of uncertain function through the walls, particularly either side of main entrances. The entrances are lintelled, often with horizontal beam sockets and a slot in the roof through the banquette above. Most have one or more such entrances of the usual height and width for enclosure entrances, but in some cases, particularly the smaller forts, a second back entrance is very small and appears to have been concealed among boulders. Such forts are found in the western lowlands south of Nyautare and in the highlands from about the latitude of Troutbeck southwards. None, however, have been recorded in the lowlands north of Nyautare or in the northern highlands. They have implications for the socio-political background of the complex.

A broad classification of different types is suggested but may not cover the full range of variation:

- Small simple enclosures, usually less than 15m in diameter, often with outcrops or large boulders inside and no evidence of regular occupation. They are found mainly from around Maristvale/St Mary's to just south of Nyautare and westwards to the Nyangombe river and may be interpreted as temporary refuges for the occupants of double concentric and simple enclosures in their vicinity.
- Larger forts with an inner enclosure of similar construction at one end. Both inner and outer walls have lintelled entrances and loopholes, and the outer enclosure could be an enlargement of the first type. There are two of these at Ziwa, one on a hill north of the Site Museum and the other on the opposite side of the valley to the west (Fig. 18). These have traces of *dhaka* house floors showing regular occupation. Pit-enclosures and simple enclosures occur close by.
- Larger single enclosures in prominent positions in the National Park area. Many of these have small stone-walled houses around five metres in outer diameter more or less densely packed inside. The largest example on a high bluff west of the upper Nyangombe valley has 29 houses within a fort about 40m × 30m. These are clearly defended settlements, more than temporary refuges for the inhabitants of neighbouring pit-structures.

- Nyangwe Fort is a unique case. Here an original enclosure has been extended by the addition of five abutting enclosures, the whole complex measuring about 70m × 60m. There is a total of at least 12 entrances and 54 loopholes. Only three of the appended enclosures have stone house circles. This fort could have been the headquarters of a chief to which people could retreat with their cattle in time of danger.
- A number of defensive sites have been recorded west of the Nyangombe river in Tanda. Several of these have a main enclosure with an outer crescentic enclosure added on one side and have traces of house floors or raised platforms within both sections. Others are single enclosures 30m or more in diameter, also with house floors. In one case several irregular enclosures are built among large boulders on the sides of a rocky hill.

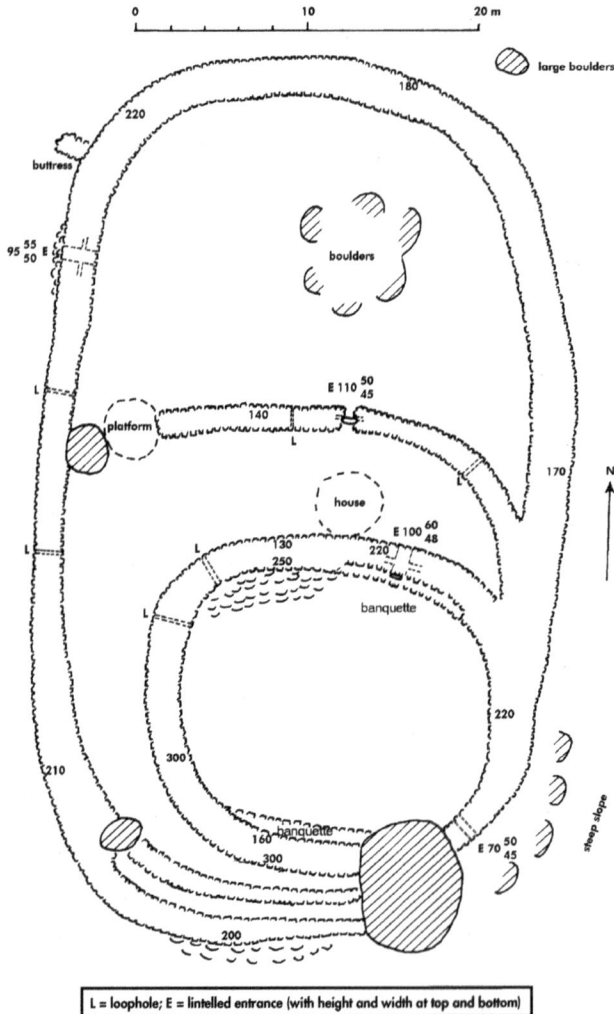

Fig. 18: Sketch plan of Mujinga fort, Ziwa

Not included in the above classification are the less coherent ruins on top of Demera Hill above Nyanga town and forts well to the south near Penhalonga. Some at least of the latter are attributable to the Manyika (as some of the National Park examples may also be).

The forts carry implications for the security and social structure of their communities. In the southern highlands the pit-structures and forts imply some social distinction. The forts were regularly occupied and thus were more than temporary refuges for dispersed villages of pit-structures. They may represent headquarters of local authority, in which case their distribution suggests relatively localised socio-political units, with a larger centre at Nyangwe. The Ziwa forts suggest a similar scale of organisation. In the St Mary's/Maristvale area the small forts without regular occupation suggest communal security measures, while to the north the lack of forts indicates greater security or some other strategy for coping with aggression.

A relatively late dating, probably within the 18th–19th centuries, indicates contemporaneity with the Manyika and Saunyama chiefdoms. The basic distribution of these larger political units does not appear to have changed much, so that the National Park forts would have fallen within the Manyika sphere of influence and the areas to the north under Saunyama. The forts would have represented local chiefs and headmen under these polities.

Defensive measures were probably mainly a response to minor inter-community raiding, while larger-scale events are illustrated by a major cattle raid by Manyika on Saunyama in the late 19th century. Ngoni raiding as part of the wider historical effects of the *mfecane* also impinged on the area in the 19th century and is stressed in the recorded traditions.

Iron working

Iron tools must have been critical for the construction and cultivation of the terraces and ridges and for building activities. Evidence for iron production is relatively common, sites ranging from scatters of slag to quite well-preserved smelting furnaces and smithing hearths. The furnaces and smithing hearths are almost always within small, roughly built stone enclosures three to four metres in diameter, and most slag occurrences are also associated with these.

There are at least three different furnace types represented among the better-preserved examples (Fig. 19). All three types are found within an area of a few square kilometres in the Nyahokwe area east of Ziwa, but elsewhere there is some hint of differing distribution. Some furnaces are sufficiently well preserved to show the remains of moulded features over the mouth. The best is in the National Park on the east side of the Pungwe valley and has small breasts, a navel and a raised belt all around (Fig. 20). Others are also likely to be female sexual symbols but are too eroded for clear identification.

Several smithing hearths have been recorded, most of them closely adjacent to furnaces, two of them in the same enclosure. The hearths are semi-cylindrical

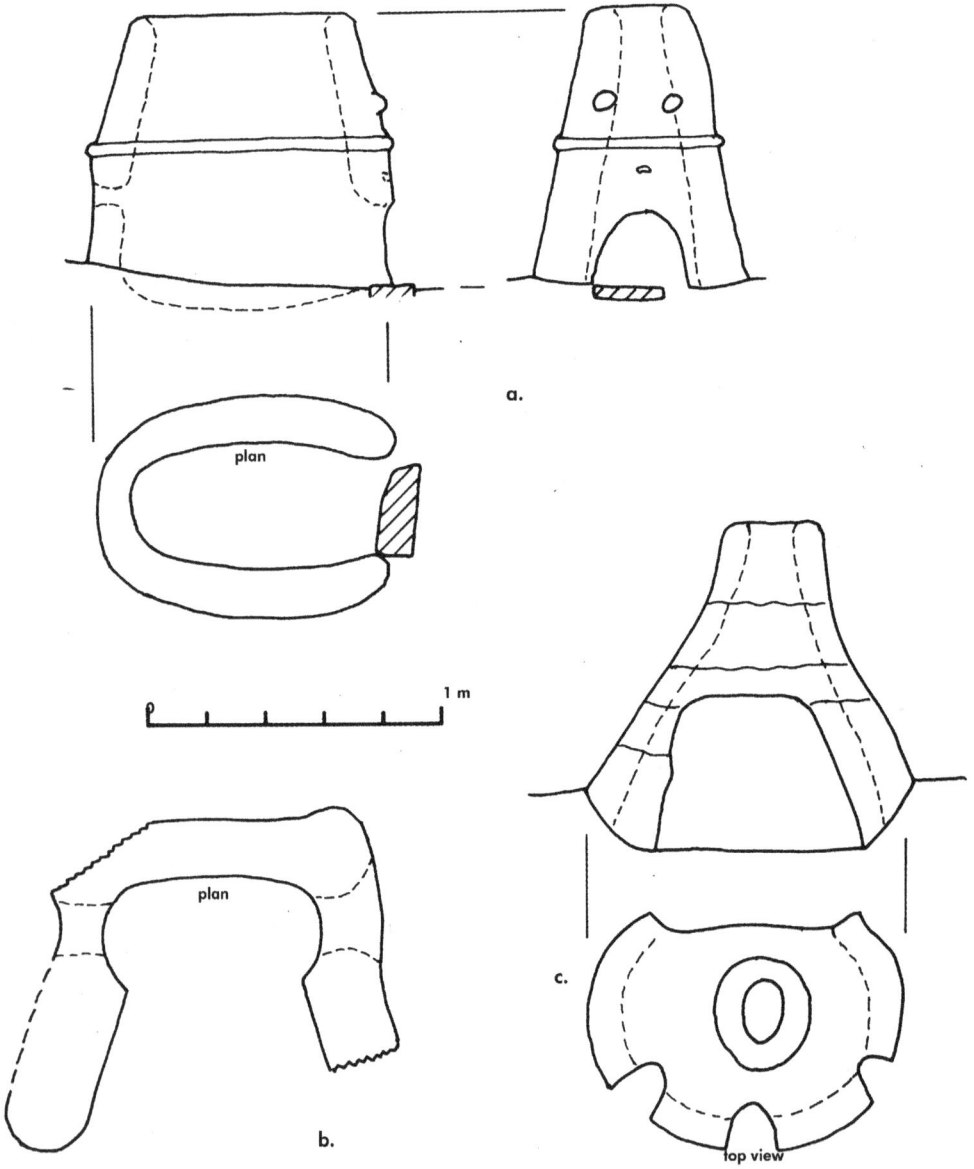

Fig. 19: Three types of iron-smelting furnaces

or horseshoe-shaped *dhaka* structures, 20 cm to 30 cm wide internally and 25 cm to 30 cm high, with traces of a hole for the tuyère (clay pipe for the bellows) at the back or side. They are associated with anvils of granite or dolerite and dolerite hammer stones.

There is little accumulation of waste slag associated with most of the furnaces, and the ore in most areas was probably relatively pure black magnetite sand that weathers from the dolerites. Concentrations of this can be seen in the vicinity of Ziwa Site Museum. However, there are larger heaps of slag in the north-east, where the ore may have been laterite. The largest is high up on a shoulder of the highlands west of Kagore. Here there is a series of heaps up to about a metre in height in an area about 20 m × 20 m, enclosing two hollows where furnaces may have been located.

Fig. 20: Furnace of type 1, middle Pungwe valley, National Park

None of these iron-working sites are directly dated but all occur quite close to stone enclosures, pit-structures or other features of the complex and it may be assumed that they are associated. Judging by the amount of slag found, the output of most individual smelting sites was not large, but the number of sites indicates an overall production that must have been adequate for the needs of the local communities. The concentration of sites in the Nyahokwe area suggests that there was some local specialisation. Iron artefacts from excavated settlement sites include a fair number of arrowheads of various shapes, small knives, *mbira* ('thumb piano') keys, a couple of axes and miscellaneous pieces. Few hoes appear to have survived but there is a chance find of two complete specimens from Ziwa (Fig. 21).

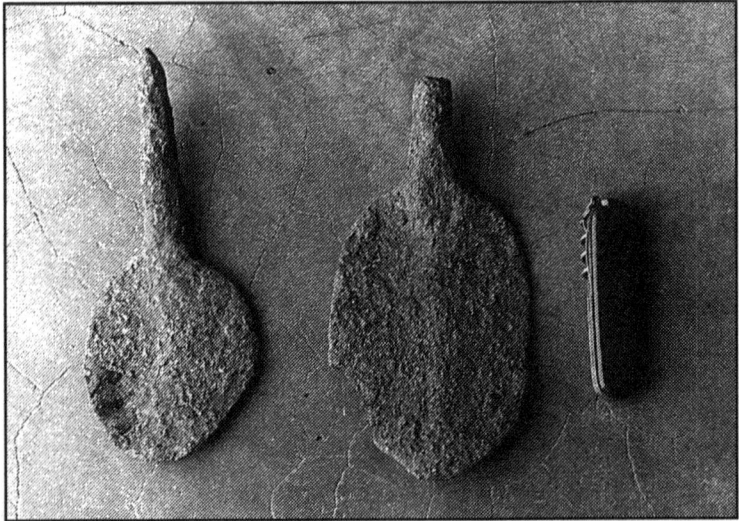

Fig. 21: Two hoes found in digging a pipe trench at Ziwa

Chapter 3
Agricultural Works and Water Management

The agricultural activities of the Nyanga people have sculpted the landscape over thousands of square kilometres, reflecting a vast input of labour invested in specialised techniques finely adapted to extract an adequate production from the potentials of the environment. The most obvious features are the regular steps of the terraces (Fig. 22). Less immediately apparent are the lowland cultivation ridges; while they show up quite clearly from the air or on aerial photographs, their scale and more subtle contours are difficult to take in from ground level. Of the water furrows, the larger ones in the National Park area stand out quite clearly, but smaller ones without substantial earthworks require a more practised eye to detect both on the ground and on aerial photographs.

This chapter will describe the physical remains, leaving the interpretation of agricultural practices to Chapter 4.

Terraces

Once the desirability of cultivating the relatively fertile stony slopes is realised, terracing with its attendant advantages is a natural procedure. The first necessity is to clear the surface stones to give scope for cultivation, and the most convenient way to dispose of these is to pile them in lines along the contour. As more stones appear and are removed in the course of cultivation, the bank of stones rises and the soil accumulates behind, leading to the development of steps or bench terraces. The soil is thus almost incidentally conserved from erosion by the checking of run-off from rainfall and the same effect allows for greater water percolation so that less water goes to waste. This simple technique has been used to good effect as a local initiative by the farmers of the Biriwiri area of Chimanimani since the 1940s. In Nyanga some of the less substantial terracing conforms to this procedure, but the majority of terracing was further developed by the construction of formal terrace walls. The former type is here called single-faced terracing and the latter double-faced.

The single-faced type tends to be found in situations where stones are relatively few and of generally small size. The vertical faces of the terraces (risers) are often fairly low, around 30 cm, and the profile of the terrace surface is sloping, with gradients of up to ten or fifteen degrees from the horizontal. While there is some modification of the natural slope, the conservation effect is limited.

The double-faced terraces are in rockier situations. Here the risers are deliberately constructed walls around one metre thick. The inner and outer faces are built from the larger rocks and the core of smaller stones. The often thin soil between the walls has been worked through to remove even the smallest stones and is almost stoneless. The terrace surface approaches the horizontal and the height and width varies with the steepness of the slope. The height of risers ranges

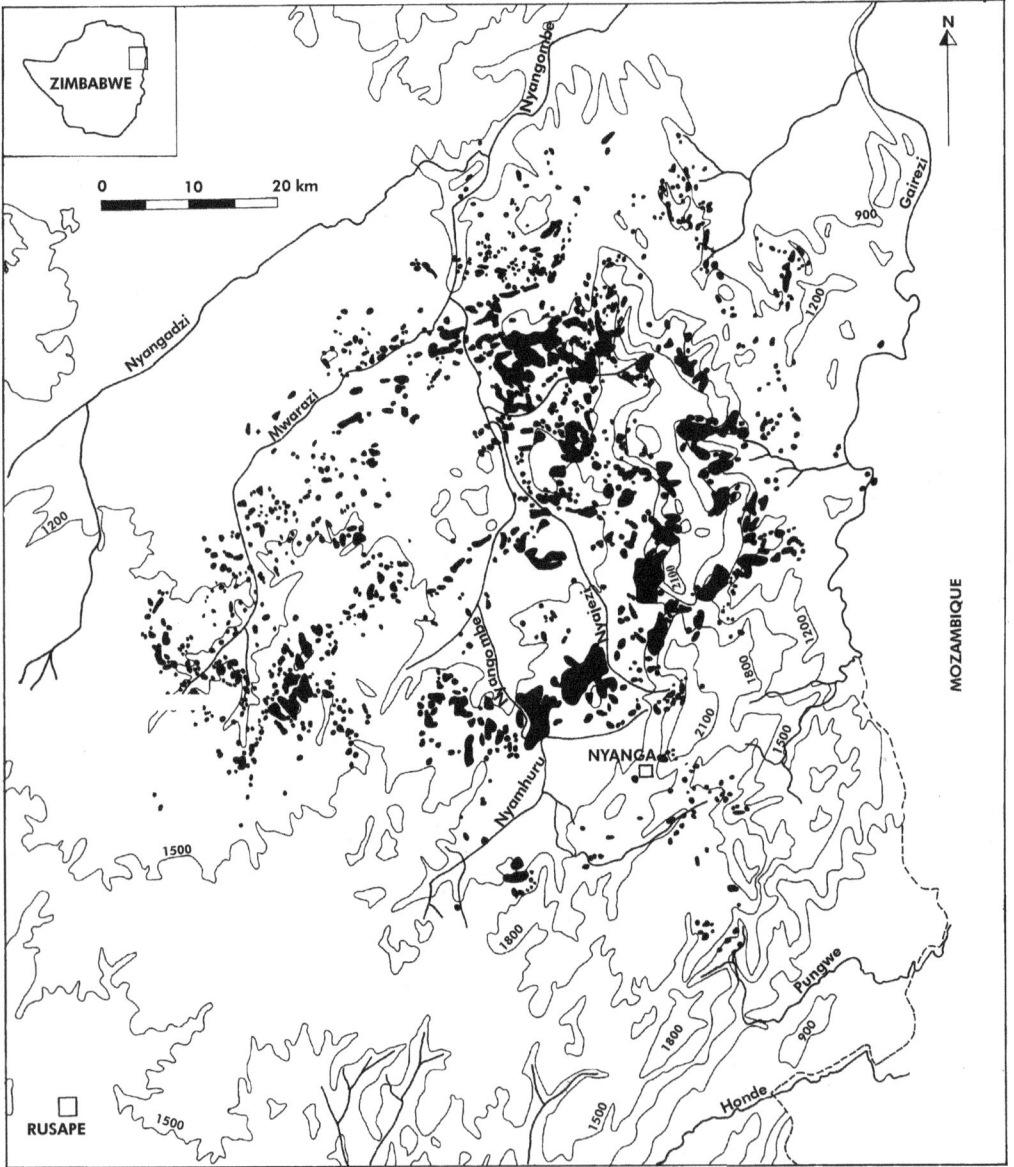

Fig. 22: Distribution of terracing identified from aerial photographs

from a few centimetres to two metres in extreme cases and is commonly around 30 cm to 70 cm, while the width of the cultivable surface (excluding the wall) is commonly two to three metres, with a range of about 1 m to 10 m. The top of the wall is sometimes flush with the terrace surface, but a raised lip of 10 cm to 20 cm is common. Where there were more stones than could be accommodated in the basic riser, they were built up into an upstanding wall which may be up to a metre or more above the surface on the upper side. Drain holes were sometimes left through such walls. Terraces were not precisely levelled along the contour, allowing for lateral drainage of excess water. Stone-lined drains in some cases direct this excess flow down through the range of terraces.

Terrace construction involved the extraction and moving of large quantities of stones, many of substantial size. In the absence of modern pick-axes, an appropriate instrument for this would be a stout small-bladed hoe, capable of working around and between the stones and providing firm leverage. A chance find from Ziwa of two such tools is illustrated in Figure 21, but hoes have not been found in archaeological excavations. Wooden levers might have aided in extracting and moving large stones, and digging-sticks could have been used in subsequent cultivation.

A further type of terrace is found on rocky granite slopes at the foot of Mount Ziwa and Hamba hill in Ziwa ruins, and on the escarpment on the south side of the Bende Gap. These are extremely roughly built, usually of large stones. Roger Summers found Ziwa Early Iron Age potsherds on the surface and in the vicinity of such terraces and considered that they could be associated. This association would be difficult to prove, since even sherds incorporated in the terraces could derive from earlier occupation. However, in the case of the Bende Gap, large fragments of Early Iron Age pottery were found on the surface in adjacent rock shelters and these would be unlikely to have survived intact had there been much subsequent activity in the area. This gives some support for the Early Iron Age inhabitants having initiated this type of terracing, although there is no reason to suppose any continuity to the later complex.

The upper altitudinal limit of terracing is at around 1,700 m with very little above this level. This corresponds to the range of cultivation of the traditional grain crops at the present day and may be controlled by climatic factors, but the leached nature of the plateau soils above this level is probably an equally important constraint.

Geologically the terracing favours the more fertile dolerite rocks and soils but also occurs on the granites and sedimentary rocks. The dolerite sills and dykes which form some of the foothills to the west of the highlands carry the densest concentration of terracing of the whole complex. Comparison of aerial photographs and geological maps shows that 26 per cent of the dolerites below 1,700 m are terraced, against only 5.5 per cent of the granites. Much of the terracing appearing on granite on the geological map is more or less closely adjacent to dolerite occurrences. Also the boundary between dolerite and granite is often not as clear-cut as the geological map implies, especially at lower altitudes where the edges of dolerite sills have been subject to slow decomposition, leaving residual dolerite rocks and soils among granite outcrops. It thus seems that terracing was concentrated primarily on the dolerite and expanded on to neighbouring granites as the available area was used up.

In the recent research a number of sample areas were selected for detailed examination, representing different geological conditions, areas, altitudes and terrace types. Cross-sections were excavated, soil samples collected, and detailed plans made in several cases.

Figure 23 on dolerite at Ziwa shows the relationship of terraces to a series of enclosures, a walled passageway and lesser pathway or drain; stone lines across series of adjacent terraces form field divisions. Figure 24 shows sample cross-sections. Soils here are red clay-loams with a subsoil of dense dolerite stones in a clayey matrix. Terrace soils are shallow, generally around 20 cm to 30 cm but often less. The tops of the riser walls form a low lip in most cases. Another sample area of similar construction at Ziwa on granite has very sandy soils, up to 60 cm deep where the gradient is relatively steep but shallower on a lesser gradient; subsoil here is decomposed granite.

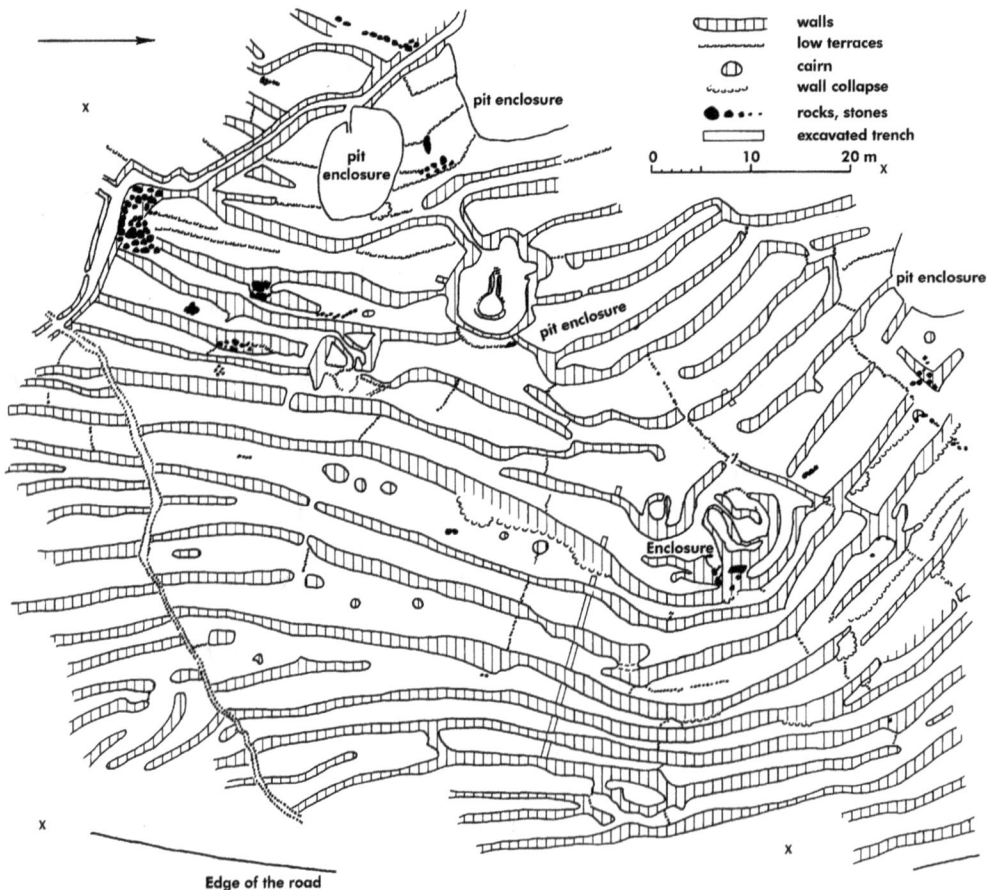

Fig. 23: Plan of terracing and enclosures at Ziwa

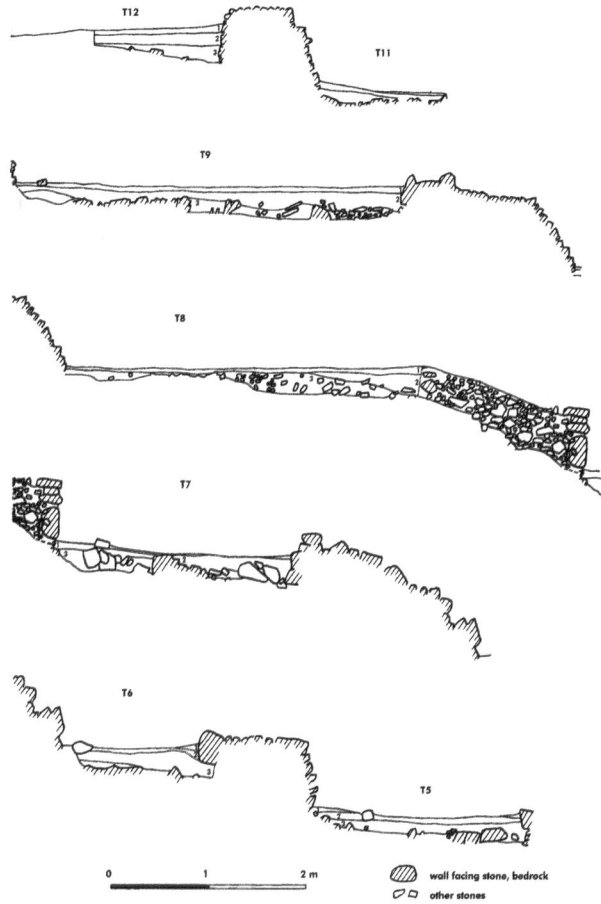

Fig. 24: Section of terrace transect, Ziwa

A sample area above Maristvale is on dolerite on the lower slope of the escarpment. Soils and construction are similar to Ziwa, but here the terrace walls are up to a metre high on the upper side and are pierced by drains at about three-metre intervals. Immediately below this site is a small, seasonally waterlogged vlei with cultivation ridges and there are a few homestead enclosures on the further side of this.

Chirangeni, north of Nyautare, is again at the foot of the escarpment, and here the terraces are on granite associated with the large enclosure described in Chapter 2 (Fig. 17). Soils are extremely sandy but relatively deep, often 30 cm to 50 cm, over decomposed granite. The tops of most of the risers are flush with the terrace surface, occasionally higher (Fig. 25). Stone-lined drains reinforce the lines of natural drainage to carry excess run-off, preventing erosion of the terraces.

The walled garden of Chirangeni mentioned in Chapter 2 is within 20m of the enclosure and slightly below it. This is an area of about 20m × 18m surrounded by a substantial wall, with three broad terraces within it. The terrace walls are mostly upstanding. The terraces are graded towards the adjacent drain, and irrigation by water spreading would not have been possible. Excavation at the lower edge of the garden showed two phases of construction: an initial single-faced terrace about 30 cm high, and a later, much larger, double-faced wall below it, filled behind with sandy soil to bury the first terrace. Small weathered potsherds and charcoal flecks scattered throughout suggest the use of domestic refuse from the enclosure as manure. However, the sherds are somewhat different from the pottery in the enclosure and could have come from an earlier site destroyed in building the terraces, while a dated sample of the charcoal also suggests an earlier date than the enclosure. There are at least two similar but smaller garden enclosures on the next spur 100 m or so to the north, but none have been recorded elsewhere.

A site above Elim Mission is on the reverse side of the sharp ridge forming the eastern escarpment. The single-faced terraces are on a steep slope with shallow, stony soil over decomposed argillite and there must have been some erosion. There are no homestead enclosures in the vicinity.

Apart from the possible Early Iron Age associations of the very rough granite type, the date of the commencement of terracing is uncertain, since dating thus far relies on association with settlement sites. The earlier sites in the highlands – early hilltop settlements and ruined pit-structures of the 14th to 16th century – are above the upper limit of terracing and no direct association has been established. Some of the ruined pits are not too far from terracing at the top of the eastern

Fig. 25: Granite terracing, Chirangeni

escarpment, but a relationship to the later pit-structures is more probable from their more consistent propinquity. Lower pit-structures within the terraced zone on the western escarpment are more confidently associated with terracing, while there is intimate association with the lowland enclosures. Terracing was thus established by at least the 17th or early 18th century, but an earlier date remains to be demonstrated.

There is no mention in the early written accounts of the 1890s and 1900s of any cultivation of terraces at that time and most had clearly been abandoned. Hwesa informants in the north-eastern lowlands state that the terraces were already there and abandoned prior to the establishment of the Katerere polity, probably between 1750 and 1800. There are, however, some hints of more recent local use, for instance in or near the Bende Gap as recorded by Stead in 1949:

> The stone-faced earth terrace is to be found on steep breath-taking slopes on the road to Nyamaropa Native Reserve via Bende. The steep slopes have been cut out into earth terraces about two feet wide and these have been faced with small flat stones which form the sub-strata of the hills. The shortage of rain in 1946–47 caused the crops grown on these terraces to be poor, but in normal seasons the crops are good.

These very narrow terraces are hardly consistent with the majority of terraces described above, while the isolated report suggests only localised use, perhaps a reuse of old terraces. Some informants in a recent survey acknowledge having sometimes cultivated on old terraces, while there has been some limited modern terrace building in Nyamaropa at the foot of the eastern escarpment. These terraces are poorly built compared to older examples, with quite steep profiles, and are designed mainly for stone clearance. In the same area, along the main road south of Regina Coeli, the current modification of old narrow terraces can be observed, forming wider terraces suitable for a plough; here both series appear to be single-faced with sloping terrace profiles.

There seems to be a common belief that terraces in general are usually irrigated, and this was assumed for Nyanga by several early writers such as Hall and Wieschoff. However, for the dense concentrations of terracing in the lowlands, gravity irrigation would have been impossible, and while there are indeed numerous water furrows in the highlands and on the escarpments, as described below, very few of these are associated with the terraces. In a few cases furrows did traverse terraced slopes en route to homesteads, and here irrigation of the terraces below the furrow is a possibility, though traces of distribution channels have not been observed. Examples are Demera hill immediately east of Nyanga village and two furrows on the lower slopes of the escarpment in the Maristvale area. There must be other instances not yet recorded but there is certainly no consistent association.

Cultivation ridges

The stone-faced terraces are not the only archaeological evidence of old agricultural activity in the Nyanga region. Traces of extensive systems of ridges and ditches are also frequent in relatively stoneless areas below the stony slopes and in the valleys (Fig. 26). Their distribution is wide and extends from the foot of the highlands at least as far as Headlands some sixty or seventy kilometres to the west, while lesser occurrences are found to the east of the northern highlands. Their extent is most easily appreciated on the aerial photographs and must be comparable in total area to that of the terraces, although no quantification has been attempted. There is, of course, no direct physical overlap with terraces, but in some cases they are immediately contiguous and are likely to be contemporary.

The ridges are roughly parallel, 7m to 10m wide between the bases of the intervening ditches, whose depth may reach up to a metre. Length depends on the topography and can be up to several hundred metres. Variations occur according to the local soils, topography and water table. The flatter, wider examples have weathered at the edges to a gently rounded shape, but in wetter situations ridges tend to be more cambered owing to the greater height and somewhat closer spacing needed for effective drainage.

These ridges are similar in conception to recent *mihomba*, a common method of cultivation of vleis or waterlogged stream banks. These are relatively short (*c.*20m–30m), straight, cambered, parallel linear ridges, usually angled directly down-slope for drainage. Indigenous crops grown on such *mihomba* in the Nyanga region are, or were, *tsenza* (*Plectranthus esculenta*, 'Livingstone potato'), cucurbits, *majo* (a plant similar to, or a variety of, taro or cocoyam, *Colocasia esculenta*), and various vegetables; rice is also reported in some areas. These *mihomba* are shorter, generally narrower, and more localised in areal extent than the cultivation ridges described here, and may in most cases be distinguished from them on the ground or on aerial photographs. They are also widely distributed throughout Zimbabwe, whereas the older ridge systems are restricted to Nyanga and Makoni Districts.

Their probable function and their siting in relation to topography vary to some extent. Some occur in vleis, areas of impeded drainage which are seasonally or more or less permanently waterlogged; here the purpose was doubtless to provide drainage and to raise the cultivated beds above the water table while providing moisture to the plant roots. However, they are equally common on sloping areas of reasonable drainage, where the purpose may have been to retard run-off and aid percolation. In some cases at least there seems to have been provision to distribute water diverted from streams or natural sponges.

An apparently first-hand tradition recounted by an old woman in Nyatwe in the Manyika area of Nyanga may relate to these cultivation ridges. She reported that gardens called *gowa* used to be cultivated in waterlogged areas (*matoro*); these were like modern gardens but had very long and narrow beds, unlike the relatively wide beds of modern gardens; they grew *tsenza*, *majo*, beans and maize in these beds. 'Modern gardens' presumably refers to recent *mihomba*, whose length is certainly shorter than the old ridges; however, the latter tend to be wider, rather than narrower.

Two examples in the Maristvale area below the foot of the western escarpment may be described.

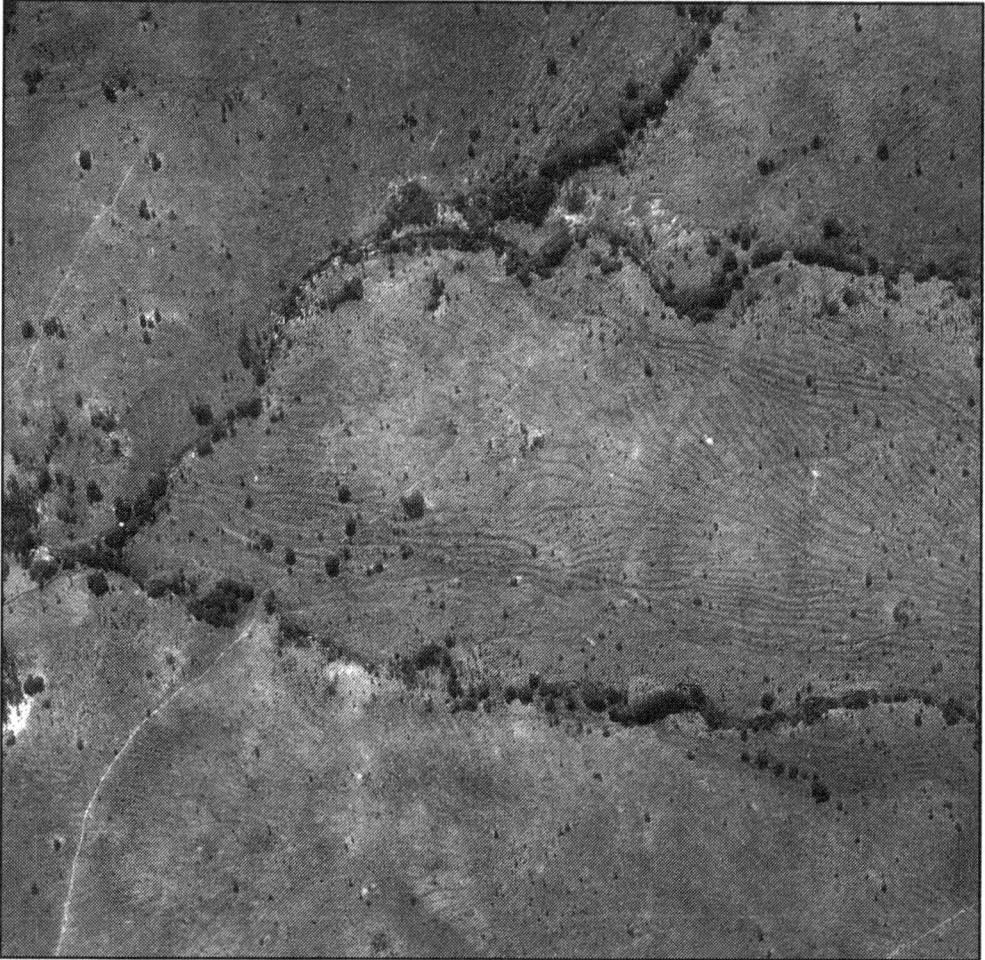

Fig. 26: Cultivation ridges north of Maristvale: aerial photograph   (*Office of the Surveyor-General, Harare*)

The first is the small, perched vlei immediately adjacent to the Maristvale terracing described above. The vlei is in a shallow valley, partly blocked by a large granite outcrop and bounded on the west by a low dolerite ridge, with a total area of about four hectares. The whole vlei has a series of ridges and intervening ditches converging to drain between the granite outcrop and the end of the dolerite ridge. At the time of study in August 1994 only the lower end of the vlei was waterlogged, but in July 1997 after a good rainy season all the ditches still retained water.

Excavation showed around one metre of mottled brown sandy clay-loam overlying a dense black clay. The rusty mottling results from regular waterlogging, and there were deep vertical cracks in the clay-loam as it dried out. The basal clay must be an original vlei deposit, perhaps water-laid, of purely natural origin, and the sandy clay-loam with occasional small stones has been deposited by erosion from the slopes above. Subsequent to this deposition, the ditches were dug for drainage to facilitate cultivation. Material from the ditches would have been piled on the ridges and alternating lenses of silt and soil in the fill of the ditches indicates repeated back-silting and recutting.

The second area is in the Mwenje basin, some four kilometres north of Maristvale Mission at an altitude of 1,360m. Here there is a broad bay in the escarpment about 2.5km wide, bounded by Mount Muozi to the south and by the Nyangui massif to the north. Streams descend from the highlands and converge in the Mwenje river, with relatively gentle interfluves between, their gradient declining steadily from the foot of the escarpment. The aerial photographs show all these interfluves to be seamed longitudinally with cultivation ridges, with a total area of over 700 hectares. There is an especially clear set of ridges on one interfluve in the centre of the basin, and this was chosen for study.

This interfluve (Fig. 26) provides an area some 1,750m long and around 500m wide, with an overall longitudinal fall of about 120m. Most of the area is covered by ridges that trend longitudinally down the spur, presenting a broadly parallel alignment, sometimes rather braided. There are some patches of low terracing along a higher, stonier crest parallel to the northern stream. A few residential enclosures are scattered the length of the interfluve, where outcropping rocks or smaller colluvial boulders provided material for their construction.

Towards the lower western end of the interfluve, soil samples taken with an auger showed up to a metre of fine silt alluvium overlying quartz gravel of an old outwash fan. Here two linear features on the aerial photograph interrupt the lines of the ridges. One crosses the ridge from side to side and must be an old trackway. The second linear feature is an old water furrow, which would have carried water to the crest of the interfluve from a series of particularly deep ditches that still carry water after heavy rain. From here it could have been directed down the north-western ditches but is more likely to have served a group of stone enclosures.

The set of ditches from which the above furrow originates can be traced continuously for the whole length of the interfluve, providing downhill access from the small northern stream at the foot of the escarpment. At this point the stream is conveniently dammed by a pair of large waterberry trees (*Syzygium cordatum*), over whose roots is a fall of 80cm providing the take-off for a shallow furrow. From here, water could have been directed to reach most of the interfluve. The stream in July 1997, after preceding good rains, had sufficient flow to supply an artificial channel, but could be less adequate in a bad year. There is little waterlogging in this area and the intention seems to have been to slow run-off and direct it the length of the interfluve, allowing it to percolate into the bases of the ridges. In addition the growing season could be extended for at least some of the area by diverting water from the stream and directing it down the ditches. The present volume of the stream might have sufficed for perhaps a couple of months, though hardly throughout the dry season. The homesteads along the interfluve could also have been served, and their distribution indicates co-operative effort for the maintenance of the system and the allocation of water rights to those lower down.

This system is admirably placed at the foot of the highlands to benefit from such supplementary irrigation. For most other non-vlei ridge systems away from the escarpment to the west, diversion of water would probably have been impracticable and supplementary irrigation is unlikely.

Water management

Much of Nyanga District – and, indeed, of the Eastern Highlands in general – is well suited to the construction of artificial water furrows, since there are many permanent streams, often with steep gradients, susceptible to relatively easy diversion. Extensive evidence of old hydraulic practices shows that this potential was appreciated and exploited. As noted above, very few of the terraces appear to have been artificially irrigated, but many of the old furrows served homesteads and in some cases irrigated open fields.

Reports of old water furrows in the western lowlands and Nyanga Police Post/ Rhodes Estate areas go back to the early years of European settlement. Furrows reported as actually operating at that time appear to have been old examples that had been reconditioned, such as the Mare furrow in the National Park, that serving the Nyanga Police Post, and another in the Dutch Settlement. Descriptions indicate that old furrows were still well preserved and could not have been long abandoned. For instance, Richard Hall (1909) says, 'They are all about 16 to 24 inches wide and about 2 feet in depth. They have no paving or built sides', while David Randall-MacIver (1906) describes them as 'simple trenches about one metre in depth. The earth taken out of the trench is piled on its lower side and supported by boulders embedded in it'.

Take-off dams in streams were also described as 'well and strongly built of unworked stones without mortar' (Randall-MacIver), and 'made of huge boulders which have been placed in position' (Hall). Such dams have not been reported since Wieschoff (1941) in about 1930, and they must have been washed away.

While most of the furrows can be attributed to the old terrace complex, the technology has continued to recent times. One informant, who was born on Rhodes Estate in 1922, remembers building furrows in his youth, while Finch (1949) records that they were in use on Nyanga Downs in 1949. Small furrows are still in current use by peasant farmers in some areas such as Chirimanyimo and the Kumbu area of Nyautare. Here they are used for irrigating gardens, household and livestock use, and in the latter case for fish ponds. This may indicate continuity from pre-colonial times or be a re-exploitation of the same potential.

A relevant tradition was recorded by Jason Machiwenyika (c.1920) in the early 1920s:

> There is also something interesting which used to be done by Manyika people in the north. They used to hoe their fields early in winter, in places where they knew water can reach easily. The fields were hoed along the rivers, and from these rivers they dug small furrows, which aided them in leading the water to the fields. Some of the furrows came a long distance to their fields. Thus irrigation began before the coming of the Europeans. They

carefully irrigated their fields in which they sowed these crops: peas, beans, pumpkins, mealies and other roots. The water ran through them rapidly and in a great volume. The countries in which irrigation was carried on are these: Nyatwe, Karombe, Nyamhuka, Bonda, Nyanga and surrounding countries.

Machiwenyika also records that men were brought from Nyanga to dig a furrow in Mutare in 1895.

It may be questioned whether an artificial water supply was really necessary, especially in the highlands, where average annual rainfall may be well over 1,000mm and permanent streams are quite frequent. However, there is great variation in annual and local rainfall so that dry years are often experienced, while rainfall is markedly seasonal and dry periods may occur during the wet season. Furrows would thus provide an insurance in unfavourable years and extend the growing season, as well as providing convenient water for domestic purposes and livestock.

Traces of old furrows can be detected on the aerial photographs. Where they involved substantial banks, as in many cases in the National Park, they are clearly visible in open grassland, but smaller, narrower examples, such as those serving groups of pit-structures in the highlands, are less easy to identify. In lower areas without perennial grass cover, abandoned furrows are more likely to have been eroded away or silted over or may be obscured by trees.

Most of the old furrows are now totally silted to a horizontal profile. They form a continuous step in the cross-slope, frequently utilised as a game trail or footpath as offering an easy route to traverse the valley side (Fig. 27). They can be confidently identified by observation of a constant downhill gradient. The step varies from a very narrow feature for some of the smaller furrows leading to pit-structures to a massive bank up to 7m wide and 2m to 3m high at the outer edge. Furrows can usually be traced back to the vicinity of the parent stream where a small waterfall often forms a likely take-off point. Some start from springs rather than streams.

As mentioned at the beginning of this section, take-off structures from parent streams have not been observed and must have been washed away since they were observed in the early 1900s. Such structures would in any case have required constant maintenance and renewal. Modern indigenous take-off dams in Chimanimani are permeable and specifically designed not to capture the whole flow of the stream. The same is the case for traditional furrows of the Marakwet in Kenya, where dams are often constructed of brushwood, impeding the flow sufficiently to direct water into the head of the furrow; these dams have to be rebuilt every year.

A broad classification of furrow types is suggested, based on configuration, construction and apparent primary function.

Class 1. Narrow furrows of varying gradient and length, directly or plausibly associated with pit-structures or other settlement sites. The longest one measured was probably 1,800m long, but most would have been considerably less.

Class 2. Generally well-graded furrows on relatively narrow revetted shelves, partly traversing ranges of terraces, probably for irrigating terraces below but also usually serving settlement sites. One example above Maristvale is 670 m long with a fall of about 27 m. Another east of Nyanga village is 770 m long with a fall of 18.2 m.

Class 3. Furrows associated with cultivation ridges.

Class 4. Well-graded furrows in the National Park and surrounding areas involving more or less massive earthen banks, rarely serving identifiable settlement sites but with potentially irrigable open areas below, sometimes with recognisable sub-furrows or ditches. Only furrow 5, which is 1,000 m long and passes above Nyamziwa Falls, ends at a group of pit-structures. The longest is 2,200 m long with a total fall of 87 m (furrow 4, see below).

Fig. 27: Footpath following old furrow, Demera hill

Class 1 would have served multiple functions, including domestic use, livestock and watering homestead gardens. Pits served by furrows would have been flushed out regularly, with the effluent in many cases impounded in basins or hollows below (see Chapter 2). If the pits were used for livestock, this effluent would have been slurry or liquid manure, for use on the homestead gardens or adjacent fields (see Chapter 4).

Class 2 is the only type which may partially support the popular conception of irrigated terrace cultivation, but the serving of settlement sites may be an equally important consideration. They form a relatively small proportion of the furrows investigated and the irrigation of terraces does not seem to have been a common practice, as discussed above.

It is not possible to generalise on Class 3, of which only one occurrence has been recognised, that of Mwenje described above. Even that may have primarily served settlements rather than the apparently associated cultivation ridges.

Class 4, although locally common, is of limited distribution, mainly in the northern part of the National Park/Nyanga town/Troutbeck area. There is no association of this class with terraces and little with settlement sites. It seems safe to conclude that their purpose was the irrigation of unterraced fields in gently sloping, relatively stoneless areas below. Traces of side ditches can be detected in some cases. These run down from the furrow at intervals of 15m to 30m; the areas between are generally flat-topped, defined by the depressed channels, and are clearly different in character from the narrower raised banks of the cultivation ridges described above. The soils here, like most of the mature highland soils, are extremely leached, only the organic carbon offering any fertility. Manuring would thus have been essential. From recent practice, it might be expected that irrigated fields were fenced for protection from animals.

The furrows are well engineered with gradients tailored to the terrain and determined by the desired destination in relation to the source. Initial courses in side valleys are generally relatively steep to achieve adequate flow of water where furrow width is often restricted by steep cross-slopes. Elsewhere gradients are rarely more than about 1°30′ and may be as little as 10′ or 20′ where it was necessary to maintain maximum height. In this steep and varied terrain the eye is often deceived so that furrows may appear to run uphill, although instruments indicate the contrary. The furrow builders would certainly have developed better judgement through experience and probably managed without any form of levelling device in most cases. In less stony situations, the flow of water under gravity would give sufficient indication, but it is hard to see how this would have sufficed where steep rocky slopes had to be traversed.

Most furrows have some degree of stone reinforcement of the lower side. On more gentle, less stony slopes this may be a single line of stones, not always continuous, set in an earth bank. On steep and stony cross-slopes more formal revetment was necessary. The best example of this is furrow 6 on the north side of the Nyanore river serving the broad valley in the angle of the main Troutbeck road junction; this crosses steeply sloping bare rock on a revetment 2m high. In some cases it was necessary to cross small side streams or drainage lines. In the case of National Park furrow 4, the stream course had been filled with large boulders through which the side-stream could filter, while in some of the Nyangui furrows advantage was taken of natural rock sills. Such crossings would have been liable to wash-outs after rain and would have needed at least annual repair. A small modern furrow in the Kumbu valley near Nyautare is carried across a stream on a hollowed log, and doubtless this expedient was used for relatively small spans in earlier times.

Enormous labour must have been expended in the construction of the large banks of Class 4, which appear grossly excessive for hydrological effectiveness, since even quite a large furrow could have been retained by a much lesser embankment. Bank construction must have taken place before the furrow itself was inserted, so that water flow could not have been used to maintain gradient. The diverging upper bank before the stream on furrow number 4 (see below) could suggest that occasional errors were made. In a number of cases the furrow ran on a narrow shelf on the outer face of the bank, a metre or so below the crest, and the reason for this remains unexplained.

An excavated cross-section on furrow 5 above Nyamziwa Falls shows a width of about 1.2 m and maximum depth of 25 cm, which had silted to about 15 cm. The gradient here is 30′, which might have given a flow of between thirty and seventy litres per second, depending on the depth of water. A cross-section of furrow 4 shows an original furrow about one metre wide and 50 cm deep, cut into the brown clayey loam of the bank and reinforced with some stones. The longitudinal gradient at this point is around 2° and it has been roughly estimated from the gradient and cross-section that the furrow could have carried 65 or 160 litres per second at water depths of 20 cm or 30 cm, respectively. This would be adequate to irrigate the potential irrigable land of approximately 10 hectares below and beyond this point.

Four examples of reservoirs associated with furrows have been recognised in the Park area. One example is 12 m long and 7 m wide, cut into the slope with a stone-reinforced bank below, and the others are similar. Their function is clearly for water storage and in two cases the water source is relatively exiguous, making storage desirable. Storage may have been temporary accumulation to provide sufficient volume for specific usage events, or more long-term to assure a more substantial regular supply than provided directly by the furrow. A similar practice is currently used in the Chirimanyimo area, where some farmers dig cisterns above their gardens, fed by small furrows, and run a hose-pipe from the base, the head of water providing pressure for spray irrigation.

The great majority of the furrows must date at least to the 19th century, but it is not unlikely that the builders of the earlier ruined pit-structures also built furrows as far back as the 17th century. Some furrows were reopened in early colonial times and are still in use. Others described here may also have been reused, especially those which still exhibit some concavity, such as parts of some of the National Park furrows. Aerial photographs taken in 1950, when many 'squatters' (indigenous inhabitants reduced to tenant status by the alienation of colonial estates) were still resident in the northern part of the National Park, do not show any furrows in active use, apart from large resuscitated furrows such as that from the Mare river serving the Rhodes Hotel. However, that photography was in winter, when there is unlikely to have been any cultivation and the furrows may have been grassed over. At that time a series of small rectangular plots and fields below a few furrows suggest reuse. The rest were certainly abandoned.

It may be concluded that there was a general appreciation of hydrological principles and the potentialities of furrow construction among the people responsible for the terrace complex, and that this was put into operation where physical circumstances permitted and the need was felt. The technology adopted was usually the simplest appropriate to the circumstances, but in the case of Class 4 was developed to a much higher degree.

Furrow 4 in the National Park is described in detail as an example of Class 4 furrows. This is the longest recorded in the recent work and is clearly visible looking west from Chawomera fort (Fig. 28). It starts at an altitude of 1,850m and the total length is 2,200m, with a fall of 87m. This probably started at the foot of a waterfall in a tributary valley, but the actual line of the first 440m is not now visible on a swampy alluvial terrace. It emerges from this side valley on a shelf about 6m wide about 7m above the stream and swings north on top of a broad bank for 300m at a gradient of 1°40′. From here the bank continues, but the furrow follows a narrow revetted shelf about one metre below the crest for another 240m at 2°30′ into a side valley where there is a small cross-stream. This is negotiated on an aqueduct of piled rocks 5m wide, the stream trickling through the rocks about 2m

Fig. 28: National Park looking north-east: Furrow 4 traverses the slope in the middle distance

below. There is a diverging upper bank before the stream which goes slightly uphill and may be an abortive line. For the next 330m after the stream there is a broad bank 2m to 3m high, but the furrow again ran on a narrow ledge below the lip of this, eventually grading up to the crest. The line then rounds a spur below a grove of *msasa* trees, and after a further 300m the bank divides into diverging lower and upper branches, with a lesser bank between. Concave furrow lines are visible on both the lower and middle banks. These banks fade out at a rock cross-dyke on the side of a spur, the average gradient from the stream-crossing to this point being 2° 13′. Another bank continues to the end of the spur at a lower level across an increasingly steep slope at a gradient of 3° 50′ and appears to end here above the Nyangombe river.

There are a number of areas of well-built stone-faced terracing, some pit-structures and an iron-smelting furnace above the furrow before the stream, and more pit-structures on the spur towards the end, but no settlement sites below the furrow. There are some four hectares of potentially irrigable land before the stream-crossing and around ten hectares below the lower course. Below and beyond the *msasa* grove are several more or less clear side take-offs from the bank. The clearest of these is stone-lined and runs diagonally down the bank, and the area below this is heavily eroded, in some places to bedrock. There are occasional shallow depressions below these take-offs but no clear straight ditches.

The proposed classes imply varying levels of organisation and co-operation for construction, maintenance and operation, according to the area or settlements served. Class 1, serving individual homesteads or groups of homesteads, would have had relatively limited labour requirements and straightforward water allocation, and suggests nuclear or extended family ownership and organisation, perhaps up to the level of a small village. Class 2, if used to irrigate terraces, might have required more formal control in the allocation of water rights and the organisation of construction and maintenance. The single example of Class 3 may also imply control above the family level for the sharing of water from a limited source, whether this was for supplementary irrigation of a large area of cultivation ridges or only for a number of scattered homesteads. The large earthen banks of Class 4 must have involved a far higher degree of labour co-operation for construction and some institutionalised control of water allocation to irrigated fields, at least at the level of a large village. However, none of the furrows described need imply any higher level of social or political organisation, and it may be noted that many recent indigenous irrigation systems in Africa are practised by acephalous societies where ownership and control is generally exercised by elders of one or more lineage groups.

Furrows and erosion

In the National Park and surrounding areas there are numerous very large erosional ravines cutting the slopes, most of them with little active erosion at the present day. Most of these ravines follow lines of natural drainage for small catchments, but others seem to be independent of this. The larger ones may be up to 250m long, 30m or more wide and 10m deep. A few are associated with old furrows which may have played a part in initiating them. The Nyamziwa furrow is cut by a ravine 40m wide and around 10m deep, cut back for about 100m above the furrow. Another case had been noticed and photographed by C. Payne in 1959 and he has also provided information on two accounts of actual gully formation. In the mid-1930s a gully was created on the right bank of the Mare river below Nyangwe Fort when the furrow which led to the Rhodes Estate manager's house burst its bank. The second case is related in the unpublished memoirs of a Mrs Filmer, who lived near Chapungu Falls, six kilometres south-south-west of Pungwe Falls, for ten years from 1937. Her breakfast was interrupted one morning by a loud roar from the spontaneous creation of such a gully, the result of a furrow which had been turned out on to the grass for cleaning, apparently overnight.

It is thus clear that these ravines could be rapidly initiated by furrow breakage. However, this would not appear to be the cause of the majority of the ravines, though human agency may well have been a contributing factor through disturbance of the vegetation cover and soil by the activities of the pit-structure inhabitants.

CHAPTER 4
Agricultural Economy

Nyanga agriculture at its height was very labour intensive in the construction, maintenance and cultivation of the terraces, ridges and water furrows. Subsistence was based on the integration of livestock and cultivation, adapted to variations in altitude and rainfall: the highlands with heavily leached soils but higher rainfall, the stony terraced escarpments and hills, and the valley areas and vleis. Options were rain-fed cultivation with or without terracing, irrigation, and the exploitation of wet lowlands. All of these seem to have been used.

Evidence comes from the fields themselves – terraces, cultivation ridges, gardens – with deductions from homestead design. Some direct but rather sparse evidence comes from seeds and animal bones, and we can assume that most of the crops traditionally grown in the region would have been available. Most of the archaeological evidence comes from the later stages of the complex. The earliest stage, the early hilltop settlements, probably saw the clearance of forests for agriculture, utilising and rapidly exhausting the accumulated organic fertility and resulting in the poor grasslands of the highlands.

Livestock

The best direct evidence for livestock, in the form of bones, comes from the Muozi ash midden, this being the only site offering substantial accumulation and good alkaline conditions for preservation. Bones from other sites comprise a few teeth and other fragments, mostly unidentifiable. Even at Muozi the sample is relatively small, and its main value is in showing the types of domestic animals present – dwarf cattle, sheep and goats. Even with a larger sample, this atypical mountain-top site could not be used to make reliable deductions on the general proportions of different animals, or on herd management practices, since the slaughter patterns may well have differed from those of the wider society.

As we saw in Chapter 2, the pits of the highland pit-structures and Ziwa pit-enclosures were designed for the penning of cattle and show the ideological as well as economic importance of these. The restricted entrance tunnels could admit only dwarf cattle but would not preclude the keeping of larger beasts elsewhere, and the constraint hardly applies to the northern double concentric enclosures or the less typical pit-enclosures which lack lintelled entrances or passages. These dwarf cattle probably represent a hitherto undefined breed for southern Africa, with relatively robust horns which would be a tight fit for the entrance passages and tunnels. There is, however, a remembered tradition that horns could be polled if they grew too long, and the same source said that the cattle had humps. That there were dwarf cattle elsewhere in the region, not necessarily of the same breed, was recorded by Selous in 1881 in Zambia just north of the modern Lusaka:

> I measured one of the largest cows (though they were all much of a size); she stood just 3 ft. 4 in. [1.02 m] at the withers. Though so small, these little

cows are capital milkers; they all had very small horns and were really beautiful little animals.

As noted in Chapter 1, the perennial grasses of the highlands constitute 'sour' grazing and lose nutritional value as they mature from May or June onwards, so that cattle lose weight. This also applies to much of the Nyanga lowlands. At the present time, however, cattle are kept year round by indigenous farmers in the highlands, often without artificial supplements, so this is not precluded in the past. Dwarf cattle might be expected to be less affected and more resilient.

In the highlands, wide pastures were available on the grassland plateaus and on any fallowed terraces on the escarpments, while crop residues on the terraced fields may have been used after the harvest in the dry season. In densely settled areas of the lowlands, such as Ziwa or parts of Nyautare, walled paths facilitated the passage of stock through the fields, but pasture may have been scarce in the vicinity of the settlements, apart from small unutilised pockets and fallow terraces. Main cattle herds, if any, may thus have been kept at a distance, as suggested by the small size of the pits or central enclosures. In both highlands and lowlands, stall-feeding (discussed below) may have eased pressure on pastures during the growing season, but forage and bedding material would still have needed to be collected.

The size of the pits and central enclosures of the double concentric enclosures should give an indication of the relative numbers kept in the homesteads, and hence perhaps of family wealth. Comparisons with the size and holding capacity of present-day cattle kraals built of posts in rural areas of Zimbabwe give an estimate for family holdings of one to four or five beasts for Ziwa with an average of 2.9 and a single case of 21. For the double concentric enclosures the figures are one to six or seven with an average of 3.4. This appears to reflect relatively low cattle ownership in the lowlands. However, even if the cattle were generally few, one might expect more variation in holdings between families. The restricted size range could rather reflect a standard practice of keeping a few beasts in the homestead, perhaps for milk and manure, while more may have been kept elsewhere, perhaps boarded out with kinfolk in the highlands. Simple enclosures with house remains but no pit or central enclosure were presumably those of families without cattle.

The pits of the highland pit-structures, apart from being considerably deeper (usually two to three metres), show more variation in size, which would suggest that they accommodated the whole family cattle herd. The estimate here is three to thirty-two beasts with an average of ten.

While some lowland families appear to have lacked cattle, most would have owned small stock. These and perhaps calves were accommodated in the divided houses of the highland pit-structures and Ziwa enclosures, incidentally implying some individual ownership within the homestead. Both sheep and goats were represented, as identified from Muozi. In the absence of such divided houses in the northern lowland enclosures, small-stock accommodation is uncertain. Goats may have been favoured in the lowlands, where more browse was available. No attempt has been made to estimate the size of small-stock holdings.

As with many African societies, sheep and goats were probably the main source of meat, while cattle constituted wealth and provided milk. The latter may only have been slaughtered and eaten in old age or on special occasions; certainly the very few beasts postulated for the lowland homesteads would not have allowed for regular slaughter. The central ideological role of cattle is emphasised by the powerful symbolic significance of the pits discussed in Chapter 2. However, one of the prime economic functions of all livestock must have been the production of manure.

Soil fertility and manure

Soils were discussed in Chapter 1, where a distinction was made between the heavily weathered and leached soils of the highland plateaux and lowland valleys, and the younger, thinner, stony soils of the escarpments and hill slopes with greater inherent mineral fertility. Highland settlement is largely on the infertile plateaux, whereas lowland settlement – or at least the visible stone enclosures – is amid the stony terraced areas. The leached plateau soils could hardly have been effectively cultivated for fields or gardens without enhancement of fertility by manuring. The younger terraced soils would have given better initial returns, but prolonging the fertility of at least a proportion of the exploited area was necessary to make the heavy labour demands of terracing cost-effective. Manure must thus have been essential.

Few sites except Muozi show any substantial accumulation of domestic rubbish, ash or dung, nor have remains of dung deposits been found in pits or divided houses. Some dried dung may have been burnt for fuel in the highlands, but this would have been less necessary in the lowlands, where wood would have been more easily available. It therefore seems that the dung was used for manure, and that domestic ash and other refuse were included with it.

There is little direct evidence as to how the dung was utilised. Fresh dung may actually reduce fertility temporarily if applied directly to the soil. Thus the accumulation and rotting of dung and associated bedding material, within the pen or on a midden, is a general farming practice for eventual spreading or digging into the soil during preparation for planting. Such a midden outside an enclosure or pit-structure would have been removed to the fields or gardens at least once a year. In the highlands the flushing and collection of slurry from many of the pits has been noted in Chapter 2, made possible by the use of furrow water where available. This slurry has a high nitrogen content in the form of urea and can be applied directly to promote crop growth. The difficulty of transporting it would have limited its use to gardens in the immediate vicinity of the homestead.

In societies where the collection of dung for manure is essential for intensive cultivation, stall-feeding is a common practice. In this practice, livestock are kept permanently penned, at least during the growing season, and forage is brought to them. Dung is thus concentrated instead of being mostly scattered over the pastures, and animals are only taken out for watering. In the case of pit-structures served by furrows the latter might not be necessary. The dung and urine are mixed with surplus forage and bedding material resulting in fairly rapid accumulation. In the Nyanga case, such stall-feeding is plausible and is supported by the very solid nature of the pens. Collecting and carrying forage would have been laborious but compensated to some extent by the saving of labour for herding in the pastures. After the harvest, stock could have been grazed on crop residues in the fields to give some direct manuring for next season.

Some very rough estimates of manure production from dung and decomposed surplus forage and bedding material can be made from the suggested cattle holdings, based on data from present-day rural Zimbabwe with adjustment for dwarf cattle. Assuming stall-feeding for six months of the cultivation season to harvest, the average highland pit-structure with ten beasts might have produced nine tonnes, a Ziwa pit-enclosure (2.9 beasts) 2.6 tonnes, and a double concentric enclosure (3.5 beasts) three tonnes. In addition, at least some proportion of the dry-season production might be expected to have been deposited directly on the fields during grazing of crop residues. At a rough estimate this production could fertilise just under one hectare per year for the highland pits, and about a quarter to a third of a hectare for the lowland pits and enclosures. This could be increased slightly with the addition of small-stock manure, and this would presumably have been all that was available to homesteads without cattle.

These amounts might have been adequate for highland families but would probably not have sufficed for more than gardens and limited infields near the lowland homesteads. Here outer fields, terraced or ridged, would have been reliant on natural fertility apart from that provided by grazing after the harvest. This fertility would not have been sustained indefinitely and an adequate area of outfields would have been needed to support a fallowing cycle, reflected in the great extent of terracing and ridging. Failing this, it would have been necessary to relocate the community, leaving that whole settlement system 'fallow', perhaps to be re-occupied and the capital infrastructure of terraces and homesteads overhauled after a suitable interval. The old broken *dhaka* incorporated in many of the homestead walls supports such re-occupation.

Crops and cultivation

Crop remains which have been recovered from archaeological excavations consist of hard seeds that have been charred and carbonised and thus preserved. These include sorghum (*mapfunde*), finger millet (*rapoko, njera, rukweza*), bullrush millet (*mhunga*), cowpeas (*nyemba*), ground beans (*nyimo*), squash and castor oil. Most of these come from lowland sites, with only cowpeas and sorghum identified from highland sites, so there are no data to distinguish any difference between highland and lowland crops – which, in any case, might be expected to be at the variety rather than the species level. These are all crops traditionally grown in the area and it is safe to assume that other traditional crops were also grown together with the useful weeds of cultivation. Such crops include other grains and legumes, roots and cucurbits.

Other traditional grains are rice and an earlier variety of maize, which seems to have been a minor crop in the 19th century at least. Roots would have been important staples. *Tsenza*, the 'Livingstone potato' (*Plectranthus esculenta*), used to be more widely grown in eastern Zimbabwe and is still popular in the Rusape area. It may be eaten raw or boiled as a rather mushy staple. Recent cultivation ridges (*mihomba*) are still sometimes referred to as '*tsenza* beds', and it may have been a major crop on the old cultivation ridges described in Chapter 3. *Tsenza* is subject to serious nematode infestation, and colonial authorities discouraged its cultivation for this reason, especially in the vicinity of potatoes.

A number of rhizomes, domesticated and wild, were also used. *Madhumbe*, the present variety of *Colocasia esculenta* (taro), is acknowledged as a recent introduction, but an older variety, *majo*, was widely grown and is still used in important rituals. The similar wild calla lily (*manzongo, Zantedeschia aethiopica*) was also eaten. Both of these are toxic unless properly processed by extended boiling, and a popular tradition recounts how they were used to poison Nguni/Ndebele raiders in the 19th century by leaving the half-processed roots out in the open for the hungry raiders to consume.

Cucurbits include several varieties of pumpkin (*manhanga*), the spiny cucumber (*magaka*) and melons. There are also a number of useful semi-weeds whose leaves or other parts were used for relish and sometimes dried for future use, such as okra (*derere*), blackjack (*nhungunira*), amaranthus (*mowa*), common nightshade (*mutsungutsungu*) and *nyevhe* (*Cleome gynandra*). Many wild plants and fruits were and still are widely used, including tamarind and baobab.

Intercropping and rotation are widely understood in African traditional cultivation, and would certainly have been practised, although not documentable archaeologically. Attendant advantages are the fixation of nitrogen by legumes for accompanying grains, adjustment of appropriate crops to relative fertility, maintenance of ground cover to inhibit evaporation and erosion, and spreading of labour requirements for planting, weeding and harvesting. Different moisture requirements of crops and varieties give some flexibility in coping with short-term rainfall fluctuation. Manuring of gardens and infields would have enhanced the benefits of these practices.

A wide range of staples and subsidiary plants were thus available. It is probable that the outlying terraced fields were devoted to the main grain staples, especially sorghum. This is supported by the lack of any traces of subsidiary ridging or mounding, associated with other crops in recent cultivation practice. The outlying large cultivation ridges would be more suitable for root crops, *Colocasia* and *Zantedeschia*, along the wetter ditches, with grains and other crops on the drier crests, perhaps including maize and rice. Legumes and pumpkins would be interplanted with grains. *Tsenza* would also have been grown here, but as a monocrop. Gardens and infields would have been cultivated more intensively with a greater variety of vegetables, oil seeds, cucurbits and some grains and legumes in case of failure on the less secure outer fields.

Technology

Narrow terraces are workable only with hand tools. Direct evidence of the tools used is sparse. Iron hoes must have been imperative for terrace construction and ridging but few traces of these have been found, apart from two small but robust chance finds recovered in the digging of a pipe trench at Ziwa (Fig. 21). The small strong blades and strong tangs of these would be appropriate for working among the stones of the terraces, but a broader blade might be considered more effective in the major movement of soil for the cultivation ridges. Hoes must have been valued possessions, wearing out quickly against the stones in terrace and homestead construction. They would have been carefully curated and the iron probably recycled. Wooden digging-sticks may well have been used for some cultivation tasks and wooden levers would have assisted in shifting large stones.

Provision for storage was essential to span the long dry season from harvest in about June to the availability of fresh produce in December or January, even in situations where irrigation could prolong the growing season in either direction. The raised platforms described in Chapter 2 reflect substantial storage capacity for preservable crops such as grains, legumes and pumpkins, while certain root crops could be left in the ground until required.

Field systems

Agricultural options, as mentioned above, are rain-fed cultivation with or without terracing, exploitation of more or less wet valley lands, and irrigation, and these are all represented in the remains of field systems, as described in Chapter 3.

The application of these is related to basic soil fertility. Younger soils of the stony slopes with greater inherent fertility were exploited by terracing, and abandoned or fallowed as fertility declined. The deeply weathered and leached soils of the highland plateaux have little potential without manuring and may not have been generally exploited, apart from homestead gardens adjacent to pit-structures, manured with dung or slurry from the pits and irrigated where practicable. Any fields for these communities must have been on the terraced escarpments, and it is not clear how they, or outlying fields in general, may have been protected from animal depredation. However, in the National Park area, where there is only localised terracing, these plateau soils were exploited with the aid of irrigation. Here fertilisation with accumulated manure would have been essential. Lowland alluvial and colluvial soils were exploited by ridging, mainly for water control, and some were irrigated. With lower rainfall, leaching is less intense and fertility might be maintained by some local manuring, incorporation of organic material in the ridges and regular fallowing. Irrigation was practised where viable with considerable skill and ingenuity, but was largely devoted to gardens, with the vast majority of fields dependent on rainfall.

Evidence for homestead gardens is reasonably clear in the radial walls of many pit-structures and in the walled plots found locally at Chirangeni, but is less clear in the other lowland enclosures. Here gardens may have been located in vleis where the water table was relatively shallow.

It is not yet certain that the large-scale ridging systems west of the highlands were developed concurrently with the terracing. None of the cultivation ridges are directly datable or have been even indirectly dated. A large-scale simultaneous use of both terracing and ridging by the same local community seems unlikely in terms of labour requirements. Lowland practice could have switched from a concentration on terracing to one on ridging (or vice versa), prompted by some climatic fluctuation. More probably, each local community emphasised one or the other system according to the predominant type of land available. Where both were available it would have offered alternative options in very wet or dry years. It may be noted that ridging systems extend westwards to the Rusape/Headlands area where terracing becomes sporadic, concentrated mainly on the limited dolerite occurrences. Thus each system was probably a parallel exploitation by related communities, each incorporating occurrences of the minor resource where it fell within its ambit.

Land-holdings

The major investment of labour in the terraces, homesteads and ridging systems implies some degree of individual or family land tenure to realise the benefits. The size of land-holdings, however, is uncertain. Some indication of terraced home fields is given by the Ziwa terrace survey (Chapter 3). Here the pattern of boundaries marked by lines of stones or cross-walls is not entirely clear but suggests a holding of 0.3 to 0.4 hectares per homestead. In this case, the propinquity of the homesteads would not have given scope for larger consolidated holdings, implying more fields elsewhere. A sandy tributary valley of the Nyangombe with ridging lies a short distance to the north of the surveyed site, and homesteads on the surrounding hills would doubtless have had plots there to expand their agricultural options in terms of crops and climatic vagaries. The two hoes mentioned above were in fact found in this valley. The Maristvale survey, with fewer homesteads in the vicinity, suggests more consolidated holdings with ridged vlei land immediately adjacent. The Chirangeni survey again constitutes a larger holding, perhaps one hectare, with the likelihood of subsidiary plots in the valley below. There must have been considerable variation in types of holdings and their distribution, according to the availability of different types of land and social factors such as local population density and family size.

In the highlands, terraced fields must have been on the escarpments at some distance below many of the homesteads, while the homestead gardens took the place of the lowland valley plots. Grazing rights would have been more on a communal basis.

A decrease in the intensity of cultivation from gardens to infields to outfields is an almost universal farming practice. Within this framework in the Nyanga case, some degree of almost continuous production from gardens may be postulated and probably annual cultivation of infields, with a fallowing cycle for the outlying terraced or ridged fields.

Elaborate 'capital' works, such as the terracing, ridging and permanent homesteads of Nyanga, have often been regarded by archaeologists as indicating intensive agriculture for sustainable long-term production from a defined area of land. Certainly we can see intensification through the development of the complex, but even at its height it is doubtful if the system could sustain the occupation of the same location for an indefinite period. Discussions above suggest that communities in the lowlands may have had to shift periodically, even if this may have been a cyclical process in the long term.

Nyanga agriculture thus developed a repertoire of specialised techniques that maintained the population as a whole for a few centuries but ultimately succumbed to overspecialisation or outside factors beyond its control.

CHAPTER 5
Society in the Nyanga Complex

Settlement patterns and social organisation

The development of the complex was set out in Chapter 2 and involves a series of shifts in settlement focus in relation to altitude and area. That this is a single sequence of cultural development is demonstrated by the relationship in pottery between the early hilltop settlements and the early ruined pit-structures, and thence by the nature of the homestead structures to the later phases in the highlands and lowlands extending into the 19th century. Consideration of the patterns of settlement at successive stages offers some preliminary deductions on relative population size and distribution, and on social and political organisation.

Early hilltop settlements

The early hilltop settlements of around the 14th to 15th centuries distributed along the crest of the northern highlands appear on present evidence to emerge spontaneously in their distinctive mountain-top situations without local antecedents. They may represent settlers from the east or north. These are nucleated villages huddled on the high hilltops of the main northern range, with populations of perhaps a few dozen up to several hundred in the case of Chirimanyimo. Total population must have been relatively small and they appear to have been isolated from much outside contact. Chirimanyimo Hill was easily the largest settlement and its special features suggest some chiefly authority. They had some livestock, probably including dwarf cattle, and must have cleared forest for cultivation around their villages.

Pit-structures

The ruined pit-structures of the 16th and/or 17th century show a change in the settlement pattern to more dispersed villages of individual homesteads within the same general territory. The locations are still at relatively high altitudes but the seclusion of the hilltops was abandoned. The downward movement may have coincided with the warmer, wetter intermediate climatic phase when a lower cloud-base may have influenced settlement. Total population may have increased but was still quite limited.

The increased size of the pits over the earlier walled hollows indicates larger family cattle holdings, perhaps associated with more available pasture land as the forest continued to be cleared by shifting cultivation. Data on relative pit size is limited, but the impression is that size was fairly standardised. However, the glass and copper beads suggest some differences in wealth; they also show developing outside contacts. Differences in the weight of copper beads between Muozi and Nyangui G7/1 suggest slightly different sources or perhaps local manufacture from imported metal.

The further downward shift to the well-preserved pit-structures was perhaps influenced by the cool phase from the late 17th century. The well-preserved pits appear to have persisted into the 19th century but their beginning is less certain. The design clearly derives from that of the earlier ruined pit-structures.

Distribution of the well-preserved pit-structures is wider than that of the earlier pits, extending from the northern end of the main highlands north of Chirimanyimo, at least to Mkondwe near Penhalonga in the south, and to beyond Triashill in the west, at altitudes above 1,400m. This distribution clearly shows territorial expansion, while the greater frequency of sites in the landscape also indicates higher population density, assuming a significant proportion of them to have been occupied at any one time.

There are a few clues to social organisation at this stage. As with the ruined pit-structures, the family homesteads were distributed in dispersed village groupings, with spacing from 30m to 100m or more. Groups of up to thirty were noted in Chapter 2 for Nyangui. Pit size and number of houses in the well-preserved pit-structures vary between and within groups or villages. Double pits or satellite pits show relative wealth in cattle in some cases. There was thus variation in family wealth and consequent social importance. Extensions to the primary platform around the pit are quite common and probably represent expanding family size, but there is little to indicate whether or not duration of homestead occupation extended beyond a single generation. Water furrows serving groups of homesteads reflect community co-operation and management institutions for construction, maintenance and water allocation. These institutions probably operated within a kin-based social organisation, as with existing ethnographic examples of irrigation systems in eastern Africa.

South of about Nyanga town, scattered walled forts with internal house circles are interspersed with pit-structures. These are likely to be at least partly contemporary and may be interpreted as refuges in time of danger, but may also represent the local authority of Manyika chiefs or headmen. Such forts appear to be absent further north. In the rugged granite country west and south of Juliasdale are numerous sites with stone walling, often with lintelled entrances, built between large boulders and outcrops with *dhaka* granaries in caves and rock-shelters. These seem to be a continuation of the Nyanga stone-building tradition adapted to new conditions of defence or concealment, a response by the Manyika to raiding by Nguni and other marauders in the 19th century. It is likely that pit-structures in this area were largely abandoned as a consequence.

Lowland enclosures

The main forms of lowland enclosures comprise pit-enclosures, double concentric enclosures and simple enclosures, as described in Chapter 2. The pit-enclosures date from the 18th to early 19th centuries, and represent a development from the well-preserved pit-structures of the highlands, with which they were at least partly contemporary. The northern enclosures, including the double concentric type, may have continued rather later, well into the 19th century, but their beginning is uncertain.

The split-level enclosures (not strictly lowland) from a limited area across the highland range just north of Chirimanyimo Hill remain undated, the only excavation having yielded little cultural material. There is no impression of any great age and they could post-date or be contemporary with neighbouring pit-structures. Similarly undated are the pit-enclosures of rather different pattern to Ziwa in Kagore northeast of the highlands and across the Nyangombe in southern Tanda; these could be parallel developments to Ziwa.

Occupation of the lowland enclosures in general is thus contemporary with that of the well-preserved pit-structures in the highlands, although the apparent development of pit-enclosures out of pit-structures would indicate that the latter started somewhat earlier. This occupation would have coincided with the last cold phase, when drier conditions may have reinforced the terracing as a water-conservation measure and perhaps stimulated the exploitation of lower, damper lands by cultivation ridges. Occupation of the lowlands might also have been expected during the preceding warmer phase, but has not been documented.

The distribution of lowland homesteads, like that of the pit-structures, displays loose clustering in village groupings and suggests that population was locally dense if all were occupied simultaneously. Homesteads in general show close integration with terracing, being often linked to walled trackways negotiating the field systems and providing passage for livestock to grazing areas and water. Cross-terrace divisions, as revealed especially in the surveyed area at Ziwa (Chapter 4), delimit areas of home fields as land-holdings, but their relatively small size implies extra cultivated land further afield, probably including a share in any available vlei land.

Homestead size again varies as with the highland pit-structures, to which can be added the presence or absence of pits or inner enclosures, with their implications for cattle ownership as discussed in Chapter 4. The standardised small size of the pits/inner enclosures suggests that only selected beasts were kept in the homesteads; this in turn could imply that more were kept elsewhere. Relative wealth is thus again apparent, while for the Ziwa enclosures at least, the non-functional aspects of design reflect availability of labour surplus to subsistence requirements, showing that this was not an especially impoverished community in general.

The duration of homestead occupation is again hard to assess, but there is little to suggest that it exceeded a single generation. Individual homesteads may have been abandoned – for instance, on the death of the owner – and new ones built nearby within the same community. However, baked *dhaka* fragments frequently incorporated in enclosure walls indicate more than one phase of house building, suggesting a cycle of abandonment and renovation of many homesteads. It is argued that this could correspond to a fallowing cycle for the terraced fields in which the whole community temporarily shifted its location. The frequent blocking of pit entrances at Ziwa and some inner enclosures further north may have a practical explanation, but could equally well be a symbolic action on the abandonment of the homestead.

The differences in homestead design between Ziwa and the northern lowlands must reflect some cultural distinction, but the pottery from each is similar, showing a close relationship.

Some of the lowland forts may represent some degree of social stratification. There are several types of forts, as described in Chapter 2. Two examples at Ziwa ruins have inner 'keeps' and evidence of regular occupation, suggesting a higher stratum of authority such as local chiefs. Most of those further north in the St Mary's/Nyautare area, however, are small single structures without regular occupation and must have been temporary refuges; further north, forts appear to be absent. Westwards across the Nyangombe are larger defensive enclosures with more numerous house-remains, which may indicate more concentrated authority, perhaps coupled with greater concern for security towards the fringes of the complex.

What were the relationships between highland and lowland communities, given the contemporaneity of pit-structures and lowland enclosures? The contrasting environments provided scope for different economic specialisations – emphasis on cattle in the highlands and cultivation on the escarpments and in the lowlands. The situation is most easily examined in the northern highlands where the escarpments are high and steep and the transition from lowlands to highlands more or less abrupt, although there is little significant impediment to movement between the two. Here the highland and lowland communities were relatively close to each other and must have had regular interaction. In addition, the close affinities between the Ziwa pit-enclosures and the pit-structures show intimate cultural relationship and surely a degree of direct kinship between the occupants. The northern enclosures show fewer affinities to the highland pit-structures, perhaps reflecting less direct kinship but not obviating co-operation.

A general scenario of mutual exchange and co-operation can be envisaged whereby cattle products from the highlands were exchanged for agricultural staples and other produce from the lowlands. Such complementarity and co-operation between highland and lowland communities is not uncommon in other parts of Africa. In addition some of the cattle of the lowlanders might have been boarded out with highland kin, at least in the wet season, when it would be desirable to keep them away from the growing crops and when the highland pastures would be at their best. It may be noted that, in the Ruangwe area at least, cattle have in recent times been moved up and down, to and from wet-season grazing in the local highlands, where they were left largely unattended. (Stock theft has now put a stop to this practice or entailed closer supervision.)

Further south, where topographical differences are not so marked, lowland resources would not have been so conveniently available to the highlanders. It may be significant that it is here that we see the development of unterraced irrigated cultivation in the highlands.

Population size and density

It is evident from the expanding geographical extent and increasing density of sites that the overall population was increasing through the development of the complex, culminating in perhaps the 18th or early 19th century. However, it seems unlikely that the total numbers were ever especially large in comparison with other parts of Zimbabwe. David Beach (2002), arguing from early colonial figures, estimated a very approximate total figure of only about 5,000 for Unyama in the late 19th century, with an overall density no higher than other parts of the eastern side of the Zimbabwe plateau (the most densely occupied part of the country). A significantly larger population in earlier times is unlikely as it would surely have attracted the attention of Portuguese observers, even in the absence of any mineral resources in which they were primarily interested. Also any substantial out-migration, occasioned either by critical population density during the complex or by a catastrophic collapse, should have been reflected in a wider diffusion of the clan totems (*mitupo*) peculiar to this area.

Relative isolation from trading activities as well as from Portuguese observers is indicated by the rarity of exotic items, limited to sparse beads, with only Muozi and one ruined pit-structure showing relative prodigality in this respect in the 16th or 17th century. A greater quantity of such items would be expected if agricultural production had been on a large scale, providing surplus for exchange, directly or indirectly, through established trade routes.

The impression is thus of a relatively small and isolated overall population which can have exploited only a relatively small proportion of the whole area at any one time. There must, however, have been quite dense *local* concentrations of population to provide the labour for terraces and ridge systems and homestead construction. Just how dense would be difficult to estimate.

The conception of a few small densely populated communities can be reconciled with the wide extent of the terracing and other agricultural and settlement remains on the hypothesis that the fields had a more or less limited fertility span and that construction was therefore an ongoing piecemeal process, with new areas being brought into use as old ones were abandoned. Eventually all suitable land available to a local community would have been exhausted and it would have been necessary to move to new location. Over a century or more, even a relatively small local population could gradually have exploited quite large areas such as Ziwa or Nyautare. On this time-scale, however, one might expect that, if the same conditions persisted, it would have been possible to re-occupy earlier settlements after an adequate period of fallow. This would have been facilitated by the already established capital infrastructure of terraces and homesteads, further realising the value of previous labour investment. Evidence of such a rejuvenation process is seen in the broken *dhaka* incorporated in many enclosure walls, representing the debris of earlier structures cleared to make way for new construction.

Burial

Evidence on burial practices is very limited, probably due to the restricted extent of most of the excavations which have been conducted. What evidence there is shows little consistent pattern. The burial in the walled hollow at the early hilltop settlement of Nyangui 1732DD27 was described in Chapter 2 – tightly contracted on its back in a small shallow grave prior to the abandonment of the structure. Roger Summers (1958) found a skeleton in a similar attitude in a small stone enclosure near Nyangwe Fort in the National Park, but its date is unknown and the site has not been relocated.

A few hand and foot bones came from the Muozi midden and would be broadly contemporary with the ruined pit-structures. Possibly the trench could have cut the edge of a grave but no trace of one was detected in the homogeneous ashy deposits.

Two burials were found in a pit-structure at Mkondwe near Penhalonga by Mrs Martin in 1936 (Martin, 1937). These had been placed in passages leading from outside the platform to divided houses and covered with 30cm to 45cm of stones and earth with fragments of baked *dhaka*. They lay on their right sides with legs flexed, and one wore an iron bangle on one wrist. Mrs Martin considered that they were secondary – not related to the original occupants – but local informants denied that they could be Manyika and it seems likely that they were buried on the abandonment of the homestead. York Mason (1933) also found some fragments of human skull in the drain of an adjacent pit-structure, as well as a shallow burial under a small cairn in the general vicinity which was not necessarily associated with the pit-structures.

The only burial evidence from a lowland enclosure is a few bones of a very young child found by Randall-MacIver in 1905 beneath an upturned pot in the passage of the small pit-enclosure close to Ziwa Site Museum (Randall-MacIver, 1906). Presumably this was beneath a blocking of the passage. Robinson found a burial in a rock-shelter on the north-western slopes of Mount Ziwa, the grave dug into late Stone Age deposits, but perhaps of later date. The body appeared to be contracted on its right side.

In several of these cases it would appear that the dead were buried within the homestead which was then abandoned. However, there is insufficient evidence to conclude that this was the general practice.

The wider context

The evidence and interpretations presented in this book have largely concentrated on the internal archaeological evidence for the Nyanga area, but they need to be understood in relation to the wider history of the region. A historical background derived from rather scanty documentary and oral tradition sources has been provided by David Beach (2002), who rightly stressed that it must be taken into account in the archaeological interpretation. However, much of this concerns the history of the ruling dynasties of polities still extant in the 20th century rather than the wider population represented by most of the archaeological evidence. The dynasties of Manyika and Maungwe and their general territories can be traced back to the 16th century and that of Saunyama well back into the 18th, certainly coinciding with much of the Nyanga complex, so that they must be relevant to a full historical picture, although there are problems with the correlation of their territories with the archaeological distributions as discussed below. The earlier phases of the complex are beyond the scope of any historical evidence (in the narrow sense) and have to be viewed against available archaeological evidence for neighbouring areas.

The complex was preceded in Nyanga in the first millennium AD by Early Farming Communities characterised by Ziwa ceramics. Such sites are found to the east and west of the northern highlands but not on the main highlands themselves, the highest site being at about 1,660m just south of the Bende Gap. The end of the Early Farming Communities elsewhere in northern Zimbabwe was around the 12th century but is not yet dated in the Nyanga area, where a later continuation is not inconceivable. There must, however, be a hiatus of several centuries to the earliest dated stone structures in the lowlands. The lowlands are unlikely to have been totally unoccupied at this time, but any such occupation is not yet documented.

The initial phase of the complex – the early hilltop settlements – lacks any known antecedents. The stone structures do not resemble any earlier remains known from this or neighbouring areas. The pottery bears none of the characteristics of Ziwa ware, nor does it relate in obvious ways to later Farming Community wares of the early to mid-second millennium, such as the Musengezi and Harare ceramic traditions of the 13th to 16th centuries found from the Harare region northwards to the Zambezi valley. If there are any connections, they are therefore more likely to lie in districts to the north or east (largely in Mozambique) which are poorly explored archaeologically. However, later cultural continuity through the complex is evident, as traced at the beginning of this chapter.

As noted in Chapter 1, the Nyanga stone structures as a whole were tentatively attributed by Summers to speakers of a language of the Sena group now found to the east in Barwe in Mozambique. He reasoned that they were built by the ancestors of the Nyama people whose language was then classified as Sena. This classification is now cast in doubt and the present Nyama language is better regarded as a branch of Shona, albeit of a distinctive form. The archaeological evidence indicates that the initial phases of the complex, and indeed other unrelated Later Farming Communities of northern Zimbabwe such as Musengezi and Harare, cannot be attributed to ancestral Shona-speakers. However, most of the peoples of north-eastern Zimbabwe must have learnt dialects of Shona by the 16th century under the influence of the Mutapa state, since early Portuguese observers did not record non-Shona-speakers in this region, although they did for the Mbara people to the west (equated with the Ingombe Ilede tradition).

The historically attested polities of Manyika and Maungwe were certainly Shona-speaking, as it now seems was Saunyama. The territories of these separate and rival polities can be compared to the 18th-century distribution of pit-structures, pit-enclosures and double concentric enclosures and their associated terracing. Typical highland pit-structures are widely distributed in Saunyama and parts of Mutasa (Manyika). Both the closely related pit-enclosures and not so closely related double concentric enclosures are also found within Saunyama, extending west into parts of what is now Makoni (Maungwe) but which may earlier have fallen within Saunyama. The split-level enclosures also fall within Saunyama. Thus Saunyama is hardly homogeneous in terms of archaeological settlement, while only parts of Mutasa are included in the complex. A simple correlation of archaeological evidence with political units is thus not evident, even allowing for some undocumented fluctuation in territories. The archaeological evidence may then be interpreted as representing an earlier substratum of communities persisting into the 19th century, on which the political superstructure and the process of Shonaisation has been imposed. The tradition relating to the Muozi site – the killing of the eponymous Muozi by Chief Saunyama – would fit neatly into such an interpretation, while some of the forts, seen as representing a degree of social stratification or local authority, could also represent this political control. Similarly the 'walled village zone' extending west towards Rusape and Headlands, related to the Nyanga complex and with historical associations with a Makoni dynasty, may also be seen in this light.

Abandonment of the complex

The societies represented by the Nyanga archaeological complex survived and flourished in a modest way over a period of 600 years by successive adaptations to a varied environment. This was achieved through the development of increasingly specialised techniques for the exploitation of the local potentials of soils, water and materials, perhaps influenced by climatic fluctuations. Such techniques included terracing, cultivation ridges, livestock husbandry, management of water and fertility, and skilful use of stone for construction. However, specialised systems depend upon a whole range of internal and external factors – social, political, economic, ecological and climatic – and are vulnerable to change in any of these.

How may circumstances have changed beyond the capacity of the society to adapt through further specialisation? Change in average annual rainfall seems an improbable factor, since they seem already to have survived the possibly drier conditions of the last cold phase around the 18th century, while the present rainfall of 800 mm or more would seem adequate. An extended episode of dry years, such as occurred on the lower Zambezi in the 1820s, could, however, have contributed to disruption. Social factors are difficult to assess on present archaeological data, but labour and its organisation is a critical resource in specialised peasant agriculture. This must have been affected in Saunyama by the extended political struggle for the chiefship between rival houses starting in the late 18th century and involving internecine strife which depopulated a substantial area of the lowland complex. Ecological decline, even if ameliorated by the sort of cyclical fallowing suggested above, may well have led to diminishing returns in the long term.

A combination of such adverse factors led, not to the total collapse of society and economy but to a new adaptation, which abandoned most of the specialised labour-intensive agricultural practices with their elaborate capital infrastructure, while parallel social changes must have eventually phased out the stone homesteads, equally laborious in construction. This may have been a gradual process continuing through the 19th century, leaving few active remnants to be recorded by the first literate observers.

APPENDIX
Radiocarbon Dates for Nyanga Sites

Radiocarbon dates as measured in the laboratory do not correspond exactly to the solar years of calendar dates. Atoms of the 14C isotope are produced in the upper atmosphere by the bombardment of nitrogen atoms by cosmic rays, but the rate of production has varied over the centuries and millennia. The 14C atoms constitute a small proportion (with 12C and 13C) of the carbon dioxide which is continuously taken up by plants and through them by animals while they are living. When an organism dies it ceases to take up new carbon. The 14C atoms are unstable and change back to nitrogen at a steady average rate, so that measurement of the remaining 14C in an excavated sample of long-dead organic material gives an estimate of the time of death. Samples from organisms living at a time of relatively high production of 14C will retain a relatively higher proportion of this isotope and will thus appear younger than their actual age when measured, with the opposite effect from times of lower production.

These differences can be compensated by calibration against the annual growth rings of trees which do correspond to solar years and hence give precise calendar dates. Sequences of such rings have been established going back many thousands of years. Radiocarbon dating of samples of known date from these sequences enables the plotting of a calibration graph of radiocarbon against calendar dates, so that the radiocarbon dates can be adjusted. Unfortunately some major fluctuations of past 14C production have resulted in S-shaped wiggles in the graph, so that at certain periods a single radiocarbon date can correspond to several different calendar dates. In the present case, this affects radiocarbon dates younger than about 400 years which have several alternative and equally probable calibrated dates.

In the list opposite, the ± figure with the radiocarbon dates is a statistical estimate at one standard deviation (a probability of 68%) that the true date falls within the given range. 'BP' is 'before present' (conventionally AD 1950). For the calibrated dates the figure in brackets is the central point and the figures either side represent the range within which the actual date should fall, again at one standard deviation. The 'most probable' date of AD 1900 is not to be taken literally, as the dates are too recent for effective calibration.

Lab.No	Site	Radiocarbon date	Calibrated ranges AD
Early hilltop settlements			
Pta-7174	Nyangui 1732DD27	590 ± 20 BP	1405 (1411) 1417
Pta-7166	Nyangui 1732DD27	650 ± 20 BP	1312 (1331) 1354; 1384 (1392) 1399
Pta-7603	Chirimanyimo Hill	530 ± 60 BP	1411 (1430) 1452
Pta-7635	Chirimanyimo Hill	720 ± 15 BP	1293 (1297) 1301
Pta-7618	Chirimanyimo Hill	690 ± 20 BP	1299 (1305) 1312; 1354-1384
Ziwa enclosures			
Pta-7161	SN153	190 ± 25 BP	1670 (1677) 1684: 1741 (1768) 1784; 1792 (1802) 1808
Pta-7155	SN153	220 ± 25 BP	1678 (1686) 1695: 1724 (1738) 1763; 1803 (1810) 1817
Pta-1191	Zimbiti Fort	200 ± 50 BP	1669 (1683/1745/1807) 1878
Pta-1595	Ziwa Fort	140 ± 45 BP	1683-1745; 1807 (1854) 1900
Pta-7067	MSE 17	160 ± 20 BP	1689 (1698,1721) 1733; 1813 (1820,1860) 1884
Pta-6410	SC12 rim of log	210 ± 20 BP	1674 (1680) 1686; 1738 (1755) 1775; 1798 (1804) 1810
Pta-5158	SC12 core of log	232 ± 12 BP	1671 (1674) 1677; 1768 (1775) 1780; 1794 (1798) 1801
	(note: most likely felling date is 1804 if the tree was c.35 years old, 1755 if c.80 years old)		
Pta-7720	Mujinga	150 ± 20 BP	1693-1727; 1816-1888
Ruined pit-structures			
Pta-7069	Nyangui G7/1	340 ± 15 BP	1525 (1540) 1560; 1635 (1642) 1645
Pta-7593	Matinha I	190 ± 45 BP	1673 (1686, 1738) 1777; 1797 (1810) 1881*
Pta-7613	Matinha I	140 ± 40 BP	1689-1773; 1813 (1884, 1920) 1939*
Well-preserved pit-structures			
Pta-7402	Fishpit	330 ± 20 BP	1638 (1645) 1651**
Pta-7599	Fishpit	95 ± 15 BP	(1900)
Pta-1412	Glenhead	75 ± 40 BP	(1900)
Pta-1549	Glenhead	60 ± 45 BP	(1900)
Other sites			
Pta-7399	Muozi midden 15 cm	265 ± 25 BP	1657 (1664) 1671; 1780-1795
Pta-7060	Muozi midden 45-55	385 ± 15 BP	1507 (1514) 1525; 1560 (1586) 1596; 1618 (1624) 1632
Pta-7400	Muozi midden 60-70	395 ± 25 BP	1485 (1511) 1525; 1560 (1591, 1621) 1632
Pta-7397	Muozi midden 80-90	520 ± 25 BP	1425 (1434) 1442
Pta-7401	Muozi midden 100-10	570 ± 20 BP	1411 (1417) 1424
Pta-7068	Elim Chigura	85 ± 25 BP	(1900)
Pta-7066	Elim Chigura	100 ± 15 BP	(1900)
Pta-7601	Chirangeni garden	200 ± 50 BP	1669 (1682, 1745, 1807) 1825; 1834-1878
Pta-7590	Chirangeni encl	300 ± 20 BP	1648 (1654) 1660**
Pta-7582	Chirangeni encl	60 ± 25 BP	(1900)

* Only the very earliest part of the calibration range appears consistent with the probable age of the structure.
** Too early for the probable age of the structure and inconsistent with other determinations.

Annotated References and Further Reading

Bassett, W. J.   1963   *A Preliminary Account of the Vegetation and Land Use in the Inyanga Intensive Conservation Area* (Salisbury, Federal Department of Conservation and Extension).

Beach, D.   2002   'History and archaeology in Nyanga', in Soper (2002) [q.v.]. Enumeration and dicussion of documentary and oral sources relevant to Nyanga archaeology.

Bruwer, A. J.   1965   *Zimbabwe: Rhodesia's Ancient Greatness* (Cape Town, Keartland) pp. 15–23, 108–12.
Narrative description of the ruins with the fixed preconception that they were built by Phoenicians.

Chirawu, S.   1999   'The Archaeology of the Ancient Agricultural and Settlement Systems in Nyanga Lowlands' (Unpublished M.Phil. dissertation, University of Zimbabwe).
Detailed description and analysis of settlement structures at the Ziwa National Monument and in the St Mary's/Maristvale area, including two excavations.

Finch, E. M.   1949   'Pit people of the Inyanga Downs', *Proceedings of the Rhodesia Scientific Association* 42: 38–59.
Very perceptive description and discussion of a wide range of archaeological features, including 'forts', pit-structures and furrows, in the area north-east of Troutbeck, based on field survey.

Garlake, P.   1966   *A Guide to the Antiquities of Inyanga* (Bulawayo, Historical Monuments Commission).
Still the most useful guidebook, competently written, mainly covering typical structures in Nyanga National Park and Ziwa [Van Niekerk] ruins. Some of the directions may be difficult to follow owing to changes in the road system.

Hall, R. N.   1909   *Prehistoric Rhodesia* (London, Unwin).
Descriptions of Nyangwe fort and stone-lined pits, with some inaccuracies and exaggerations. Convincingly refutes Randall-MacIver's (1906) claim that the Nyanga ruins are identical with the Great Zimbabwe tradition.

Machiwenyika, J.   c. 1920   'History and Customs of the Manyika' (Unpublished manuscript). Relevant parts quoted in Beach (2002) [q.v.].

Martin, C.   1937   'Prehistoric burials at Penhalonga', *South African Journal of Science* 33: 1037–43.
Two burials from passages to hut circles in a pit-structure and a third from a cairn excavated by Mason (1933). Suggests that the former are secondary.

Mason, A. Y.   1933   'The Penhalonga ruins, S. Rhodesia', *South African Journal of Science* 30: 559–81.
Describes stone structures at Mkondwe, including ancient and recent forts, terracing, water furrows and especially pit-structures, through one of which a complete cross-section was excavated.

Mullan, J. E.   1969   *The Arab Builders of Zimbabwe* (Umtali, J. E. Mullan).
Attributes the Nyanga ruins to Yemeni Arabs, with a confused understanding of the archaeological evidence.

Peters, C.   1902   *The Eldorado of the Ancients* (London, Pearson).
Peters passed down the western side of the highlands in August 1901, when the area
from Nhani to Inyanga Police Camp was apparently totally depopulated. He mentions or
describes, not very clearly, terraces, enclosures, furrows and pit-structures, speculating
that the latter were mine shafts and for gold washing, and that all show Semitic influence.

Randall-MacIver, D.   1906   *Mediaeval Rhodesia* (London, Macmillan), 1–37.
Includes the first archaeological investigation of the ruins. Describes four forts, a pit-
structure and water furrows on Rhodes Estate [National Park] and the stone ruins
and Early Iron Age 'Place of Offerings' at Van Niekerk [Ziwa] ruins (thought to be
contemporary). Photographs and plans of sites and finds.

Schlichter, H.   1899   'Travels and researches in Rhodesia', *Geographical Journal*
13(4): 376–96.
Like Peters, Schlichter passed southwards through the western lowlands to Nyanga
Police Post. He enthuses about, but does not describe, terraces (regarded as recent),
and 'ancient' forts, slave pits, large aqueducts, smelting furnaces, extensive citadels and
an 'ancient Semitic inscription'. The whole paper is full of unsubstantiated assertions. His
idea of a direct analogy is that Great Zimbabwe and Solomon's temple were both built of
unhewn stones.

Selous, F. C.   1881   *A Hunter's Wanderings in Africa* (London).

Soper, R.   2002   *Nyanga: Ancient Fields, Settlements and Agricultural History
in Zimbabwe* (Nairobi, The British Institute in Eastern Africa).
Presents the archaeological evidence in detail with more extensive discussion of
interpretations.

Stead, W. H.   1949   'The people of early Rhodesia', *Proceedings of the Rhodesia
Scientific Association* 42: 75–83.
Reasoned interpretation of terraces and pits, concluding not too dogmatically that they
were built under Arab influence to grow wheat for Sofala, the pits being either to protect
grain-bins or as sheltered dwellings. Records the current cultivation of narrow terraces in
Bende in the 1940s and the reuse of pits as cattle kraals.

Stocklmayer, V. R.   1978   *The Geology of the Country around Inyanga*
(Rhodesia Geological Survey Bulletin, 79).

1980   *The Geology of the Inyanga North–Makaha Area*
(Zimbabwe Geological Survey Bulletin, 89).

Summers, R.   1958   *Inyanga: Prehistoric Settlements in Southern Rhodesia*
(Cambridge, Cambridge University Press).
Definitive monograph on his and Robinson's research from 1949 to 1951, with sections on
beads (Schofield), bones (Cooke) and botanical notes (Wild). Describes the structures,
excavations and finds, with perceptive interpretation and synthesis.

Sutton, J.   1983   'A new look at the Inyanga terraces', *Zimbabwean Prehistory*
19: 12–19.
A thoughtful description and discussion of the terraces from the point of view of an
extensive agricultural system, with consideration of the role of irrigation.

1988   'More on the cultivation terraces of Nyanga: The case for cattle
manure', *Zimbabwean Prehistory* 20: 21–4.
Reconsiders the terraces as possibly a more intensive agricultural system using manure
from stall-fed cattle.

1989   'Towards a history of cultivating the fields', *Azania* 24: 99–112.
Wide ranging review of 'specialised' agricultural techniques with frequent references to
Nyanga on aspects of terracing, ridging, irrigation, manuring and settlement patterns.

Whitlow, R.   1983   'Vlei cultivation in Zimbabwe: Reflections on the past – a play
with a difference', *Zimbabwe Agricultural Journal* 80(3): 123–135.

Whitty, A.   1959   'A classification of prehistoric stone buildings in Mashonaland,
Southern Rhodesia', *South African Archaeological Bulletin* 14, 54: 57–71.
A classification for Mashonaland in general. Rather general on Nyanga but recognises a
'surprisingly sophisticated' and realistic attitude to building compared to the 'conceptually
primitive' stone architecture of Great Zimbabwe.

Wieschoff, H. A.   1941   *The Zimbabwe–Monomatapa Culture in South-east
Africa* (Menasha [Wisconsin], G. Banta). pp. 23 ff.
Belated publication of work on Frobenius's expedition in 1929. Describes terraces,
furrows and pits, not always entirely accurately, interpreting the pits as dwellings. Gives
the first description of 'double concentric enclosures'. Excavation of the Khami phase site
of Niamara east of Nyanga in Mozambique, and description of ruins in Maungwe north-
east of Rusape.

www.ingramcontent.com/pod-product-compliance
Lightning Source LLC
Chambersburg PA
CBHW080254030426
42334CB00023BA/2811